PRESERVATION POLICIES AND CONSERVATION IN BRITISH LIBRARIES:

REPORT OF THE CAMBRIDGE UNIVERSITY LIBRARY CONSERVATION PROJECT

Concinnator librorum. Buchbinder.

Quisquis in Aonijs studiosus obambulat hortis,
Et studijs tempus mitibus omne locat.
Huc properet, vigili ferat atq; volumina dextra,
Edita Calcographus quæ prius ære dedit.

Hic ego campactos tibi leuigo ritè libellos,
Et polio, picta postmodo pelle tego.
Sericeis etiam ligis operosus adorno,
Atq; com.is, summa qua decet arte seco.
Inter ut Aonidum vel mille volumina pulchrè
Emineat cultu conueniente liber.

Jost Amman's Buchbinder, 1568.

PRESERVATION POLICIES AND CONSERVATION IN BRITISH LIBRARIES:

REPORT OF THE CAMBRIDGE UNIVERSITY LIBRARY CONSERVATION PROJECT

F W RATCLIFFE
with the assistance of
D PATTERSON

Library and Information Research Report 25

Abstract

The Cambridge Conservation Project had two immediate objectives: to establish the facts about preservation policies and practices in libraries in the UK and to identify the educational and training facilities available to librarians and practitioners. Nationwide surveys by questionnaires, interviews and seminars were among the methods used. On both counts the findings were conclusive.

With regard to the former, whilst preservation awareness is growing in libraries of all kinds, few libraries have preservation policies and, of those, only the largest can afford to pursue them in any realistic sense. Moreover, there is no national plan or even the makings of one: there are virtually no resources available to meet the need. In regard to education and training, the situation is even worse. Preservation is not included in library school curricula and the opportunities for the training of binders and conservators are plainly inadequate.

The report makes recommendations for action in two areas, first within individual libraries, involving little or no additional expenditure and immediately applicable, secondly at a national level. Among the latter, the twin needs for cooperative action, for which no mechanism exists at present, and for a focal point for preservation, some sort of National Advisory and Research Centre, are of prime importance. The status, funding and location of the latter needs further clarification but involvement of the British Library in any such undertaking seems essential to its success.

The importance of cooperation with other interested parties, archivists, the book trade, the paper and printing industries and scientific research is also emphasised. A decisive contribution to the preservation problem would result from the use of acid-free paper and durable bindings in book production. The continuing involvement of LISC in promoting a national preservation policy should be sought, in order to sustain the momentum of the present research and the interest and awareness growing in libraries.

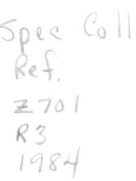

British Library Cataloguing in Publication Data

Ratcliffe, F.W.
 Preservation policies and conservation in British libraries. – (Library and information research reports, ISSN 0263-1709; 25)
 1. Library materials – Great Britain – Conservation and restoration
 I. Title II. Patterson, D. III. Series 025.8'4'0941 Z701
 ISBN 0-7123-3035-6

Library and Information Research Reports are published by the British Library and distributed by Publications Section, British Library Lending Division, Boston Spa, Wetherby, West Yorkshire LS23 7BQ.

© The British Library Board 1984

ISBN 0 7123 3035 6
ISSN 0263 1709

The opinions expressed in this report are those of the authors and not necessarily those of the British Library.

Typeset and printed in Great Britain by Cambridge University Printing Services on neutral-sized paper.

Contents

Page

Preface		ix
Project Steering Committee		xi
Acknowledgements		xii
1	**Introduction**	1
1.1	The problem	1
1.2	The evidence	1
1.3	The library position	2
2	**Background to the project**	4
2.1	The awakening	4
2.2	Technical skills	4
2.3	Library problems	5
2.4	Symptoms	5
2.5	Awareness	6
3	**Objectives**	8
3.1	Formulation of objectives	8
3.2	Limitations	9
4	**Method**	10
4.1	Experience	10
4.2	Contacts	10
4.3	Preliminary survey	11
4.4	Pilot questionnaire	12
4.5	Main questionnaire	13
5	**Questionnaire to libraries**	16
5.1	The returns	16
5.2	The findings	17
5.3	Discussion	20
6	**Questionnaire on training: findings and discussion**	25
6.1	The returns	25
6.2	The findings and discussion	25
6.3	Training courses	27
6.4	Manpower problems	28
6.5	Preservation problems	30
6.6	Short courses	30

7	**Microforms and non-book media**	31
7.1	The present situation	31
7.2	Microform conservation	32
7.3	Current use	33
7.4	National Reprographic Centre for documentation	33
7.5	The future	34
8	**National Advisory and Research Centre**	36
8.1	Need	36
8.2	Status of the centre	37
8.3	Location	38
9	**Priorities and policies**	39
9.1	Expenditure	39
9.2	Ordering priorities in 'binding'	42
9.3	Collection building	43
9.4	Local considerations	44
9.5	Staff requirements	44
9.6	National heritage	45
10	**International perspective**	47
10.1	The Canadian survey	47
10.2	The Australian scene	48
10.3	Awareness	49
10.4	An American perspective	51
11	**Conclusions**	52
11.1	The preservation position	52
11.2	Unpreparedness	53
11.3	Policy matters	54
12	**Recommendations**	56
12.1	Recognition of the problem	56
12.2	Executive action: local strategy	56
12.3	Priorities within the library	59
12.4	National cooperative possibilities	61
12.5	The trade and industry	63
12.6	New media	65
12.7	Environmental conditions	66
12.8	National Advisory and Research Centre	66
12.9	The solution	67
12.10	Summary of recommendations	68
	12.10.1 Activities within individual libraries	68
	12.10.2 Cooperative activities	69

13 References	70
14 Glossary of conservation terms	73
Appendix 1 – The questionnaires	76
Appendix 2 – Conservation policies and activities in national libraries: synopsis of Canadian survey	81
Appendix 3 – Papers submitted by committee members to the Project Steering Committee, 7 April 1982	83
Appendix 4 – Papers read at the Cambridge Dissemination Seminar, 22 September 1983	99
Other reports	132

Preface

One almost feels that this report should be prefaced with a warning that some readers might find the contents distressing; certainly its findings will come as a shock to many readers, not a few librarians and many lay governors of libraries among them. Dr Ratcliffe has amply achieved his purpose of establishing factually and on a national basis the current policies and practices of libraries in regard to the conservation and preservation of their materials, also the state of the trades and professions which exist to serve them. He has set these resources in the context of the problems, as revealed in the literature and in the important contributions which he has elicited from a number of expert witnesses.

This report, even in the course of its preparation, made a significant contribution to raising awareness of the scale of the threat to recorded knowledge represented by wear and tear, unsuitable environments, and the inherent instability of materials in modern publications. That awareness is beginning to change general indifference to quiet concern and self-questioning among administrators of libraries, with whom responsibility mainly lies. A Great Debate must follow to establish a general professional position on the new priority to be given to preservation, in competition with the need to develop collections and to take advantage of new technology in exploiting them, and in the face of seriously reduced resources.

Obviously the balance must differ in libraries of various types: national and other research libraries will have a different view from that of a public library system, whilst the head of an information centre, depending more and more heavily upon electronic information, may feel that printed materials are expendable.

But every library of significance is a library of record, e.g. public libraries have local studies collections which form a unique part of the national archive. Again, the librarian who says, quite properly, that his particular collections are for use and subject to rapid turnover, so that his only concern is a business-like one to ensure that the materials last as long as he has use for them, has at least the duty to establish systematic procedures and to allocate adequate resources. Unfortunately, the report reveals that few libraries have a methodology for systematic screening of their collections and for conservation management. There is a vicious circle, whereby the practising element of the profession has neglected collection maintenance, the library schools have taken their cue in concentrating upon the use of new technology for library housekeeping and for information provision, squeezing out in the process that consideration of the physical book which has been regarded as redundant to the young professional librarian of these past 20 years. Consequently, middle and junior management in our libraries are often ignorant of the book as artefact and the vicious circle is completed by that lack of concern for the management of the collections to which one has referred.

Dr Ratcliffe divides his recommendations into those for attention by individual institutions and those which require cooperation or central action. Clearly, it is a change of attitude and practice at the local level which can have the greatest beneficial effect. Even a small switch of resources into conservation and preservation can achieve a greater total impact than the most generous infusion of resources centrally, desirable as the latter may be. The first step is to be convinced, the second is to understand one's own position and the third is to enter into cooperative ventures, making national preservation policy complementary to the growing moves towards national acquisitions policy. Curiously enough, the new technology, which has in one sense diverted librarians from preservation problems, offers one major hope for preservation through such media as archival-quality microfilm and, in future, the optical digital disc. Also, we need to remember that non-print media have problems of conservation much worse than print. To the computer world, 'archival' means lasting 10 years or so.

To the British Library, having gone through the stages of horrified awareness, survey, rapid build up of resources, it is all too clear that the final stage of cooperative action is upon us, and that national and international projects should be mounted when other libraries are ready to join us.

Members of the Steering Committee of the project would, I am sure, share my admiration for the dedication and thoroughness with which the Project Director and Research Assistant have tackled their massive task. The report deserves the most careful study by all professional librarians and its conclusions ought to be drawn to the attention of the governors and users of libraries everywhere. We are also appreciative of the fact that the British Library Research and Development Department is now giving attention to conservation and preservation.

Alex Wilson

Project Steering Committee

A Wilson (Chairman)
N Barker
L Bell
B C Bloomfield
B L Enright
B G Gowenlock
N Pickwoad
D L Thomas
W G Thompson
M L Turner
F W Ratcliffe (Project Director)
D Patterson (Research Assistant)
M H O'Hare (British Library Research and Development Department Staff)
T C Bomford (Project Liaison Officer)

Acknowledgements

This project would not have been undertaken without the encouragement and funding of the British Library. Preservation is clearly high among its priorities and it is a pleasure to record my thanks for making the project possible and in particular to the Research and Development Department for all its assistance and ready support. The members of the Project Steering Committee were utterly committed to the project and were of immense value to the Project Director throughout. Special thanks must be made to them and particularly to Alex Wilson, who willingly shouldered the Chairmanship and was drafted into chairing seminars and a variety of other activities without complaint. The project could not have been carried through without the cooperation of numerous librarians in a variety of libraries and many staff in library schools, colleges of technology and other institutions of higher education who endured the questionnaires and enquiries from Miss Patterson and myself. Not least are my thanks to the staff in my own library, who have played their part in bringing this project to a successful conclusion.

F W Ratcliffe

1 Introduction

1.1 The problem

Conservation has emerged as a major new theme in the librarianship of today. In the context of the growth of new technology that might seem surprising, so many facets of library life having been affected by computer applications. In the larger context of library history, it might seem simply improbable. After all, the preservation, conservation and restoration of library materials has been a necessary preoccupation for those disseminating and storing information since that practice began. To Jost Amman[1] in 1568 the 'Buchbinder' represented just one of those technical skills or crafts portrayed in his *Panoplia*. In 1982 the French magazine *Figaro*[2] published an article on 'l'art presque oublié de la reliure'.

More accurately, conservation awareness has become a major new theme in libraries and their administration. Library reports, the professional literature, conferences for librarians and the book trade have referred increasingly to the problem. This British Library report was commissioned to find out the facts, since no body of hard evidence seemed to exist. The general comment about the needs and the possible impending disasters facing libraries has been taken for fact.

1.2 The evidence

This report, therefore, is concerned to examine the extent and reality of conservational need: it is not primarily concerned with the scientific or technical aspects of conserving the materials themselves. The latter has been and is the object of much research in the UK and abroad and there is already much information available. In fact, there is a remarkable contrast between the level of conservation technical expertise and the knowledge of library requirements. The Cambridge 1980 Symposium[3], for example, brought into focus the extensive range of technical expertise and scientific knowledge which exists internationally. It also underlined how little this scholarly progress and scientific research impinges on libraries. A paper[3] produced early in the preparation of this report emphasised the absence of communication between scientists, engaged in research directly applicable to conservation, and librarians; it suggested that research directly relevant to libraries was carried out without reference to libraries, almost oblivious to library needs. That librarians in this country should not be conversant with the work being carried out at the Institut für Buch- und Handschriftenrestaurierung in Munich, or even at the Preservation Office in the Library of Congress is one thing. That they should be, by and large, unaware of the work being done by the Society of Archivists, the Institute of Paper Conservation and the British Leather Manufacturers' Research Association among others concerned with the conservation of library materials in Britain, is another thing altogether.

It is not proposed to discuss in any depth either conservation in its historical context or its treatment in the professional literature. It suffices to refer to the valuable accounts and bibliographies by P N Banks[4] and, most recently published, G M and D G Cunha[5]. There are, however, interesting pointers to the situation of another, albeit negative, kind which may be referred to briefly. Keyes D Metcalf[6] in his still essential book on library planning published in 1965 made no direct reference to any provision for conservation needs even in the context of the humidity problems in buildings. He did note a trend to discontinue in-house binderies in favour of using external firms in the USA, but essentially as a planning consideration. Two years later the Parry Report[7] mentioned air-conditioning, temperature, humidity controls and microforms as important elements in preservation. In a work of its size and influence, the brevity of the references hardly identifies conservation as a major theme. The total expenditure on 'binding' for all university libraries in Great Britain, quoted in the report from the returns of the University Grants Committee for 1964/5, was £292,865 out of a total spending of £4,813,092, that is about 6%, or as a proportion of the expenditure on books and periodicals, £1,757,459, almost 16½%. Another sort of pointer is that the Library of Congress formally established its Preservation Office as recently as 1972, although the post of Assistant Director for Preservation already existed. By 1980 it had a National Preservation Program Officer with an Ad Hoc Advisory Committee and today there is a National Preservation Office in the Library. The British Library Reference Division appointed its first Head of Conservation in 1976. The importance of this development has been marked further this year, 1983, by the creation within the Reference Division of a Keepership for Preservation, thus elevating the post to the level of those responsible for other principal activities of the Division. In the words of the job advertisement, this new post 'has been established to control planning and implementation of the technical processes of preservation and transfer of material from one medium to another, including management of research and of consultative services; training; and scholarly investigation into materials and printing'. The wide brief underlines the growth and extent of the concern within the Library.

1.3 The library position

Preservation in Britain has only recently assumed importance in library administration. Part of the answer to this apparent neglect must rest in terminology. Preservation, conservation, restoration, in that order, are three ingredients in one process and in some respects they are still relatively new concepts in British librarianship. Until comparatively recent times, binding was the omnibus library term used to encompass all conservation work and this activity has long been with us. In some libraries it has stood as a separate head in the budget, more often it has been subsumed in consumables, equipment and, not infrequently, not featured at all. This is in marked contrast to the approach to, and handling of, the situation by archivists who have encountered the same problems. Many of the conservation techniques, so applicable to, and now so necessary in, libraries have long been implemented by, and to some extent pioneered by, this closely related profession. For librarians, the subject with all its implications has only truly come alive, both nationally and internationally, within the last decade, more precisely in Britain during the last five years. It has arrived with every possible prognostication of disaster. Since it impinges on virtually every facet of librarianship, if accorded an appropriate order of priority, this points to development, and consequently costs, of a magnitude which put even those of automation into a new perspective.

It follows that this report is aimed first and foremost at librarians, at the library profession, not at the conservators or the practitioners at the bench, important to them though it may be. It seeks to bring the issues before those who control library policy and library funds; before librarians at all levels and in all areas of library activity, who should be acquainted with and have concern for the long-term welfare of their library; and not least before the professional educators in library schools. The report examines national requirements and the possibility of bringing existing resources and technical expertise into a coordinated pattern of conservation in libraries. It is concerned with current practices and future policies.

2 Background to the project

2.1 The awakening

The disaster in Florence[8] in early November 1966 left its mark on more than library stock. A catastrophe of national proportions in Italy triggered off an international response. It revealed not only the limitations which circumscribed national action but also the comparatively limited number of rescue options open to libraries. Book production may have advanced a long way as far as mechanisation went, but the salvage of damaged materials, immediate treatment and restorative measures seemed at first to have changed little since the invention of printing. Quite simply, despite centuries of experience of disasters large and small, there was no immediate plan of action available to meet the emergency, certainly no 'disaster planning' as such. Moreover, although there were the traditional binder craftsmen, who made a vital contribution in the subsequent operations, there were few with the appropriate scientific knowledge, conservators of the kind which librarians are now beginning to know.

This was a crucial event, a catalyst in a situation which many other factors were identifying in less dramatic ways. The real impact of the introduction of wood pulp in paper production during the last century, the high incidence of acidity in paper so deleterious in the conservation of books, although well-known for a long time, has been recognised by the library profession at large in the UK as an urgent problem only in the post-1945 period. Its recognition as a major threat to stock coincided with the building of many libraries. These brought new standards of lighting and heating, possibly advantageous to users but of very doubtful value to books. Now, many of those problems experienced much earlier in the USA began to occur in the UK also. The great upsurge in use of libraries by readers during this time, an inevitable corollary to the expansion in higher education and increased leisure, constituted a new hazard in the control, use and preservation of stock. It placed an unprecedented order of demand on services and stock, bringing pressure in the use of primary and secondary research materials of a kind not experienced hitherto.

2.2 Technical skills

The post-war period has also witnessed social changes reminiscent in some ways of the flight of farm workers from the country during the Industrial

Revolution. Skilled craftsmen have sought higher rewards in other, usually less demanding and certainly less skilled, work. The well-tried apprenticeship schemes changed their outlook and their form too and in the overwhelming emphasis on the benefits of education, much motivation to work in traditional crafts was lost. It seems much more acceptable to the school-leaver to seek a career in keypunching at a terminal linked to a computer than to become a forwarder or finisher at a bench in a bindery. The demise of binding shops in towns and cities can be traced through auction catalogues throughout this period. No less crucial were the changes in publishers' bindings, the spread of the so-called 'perfect binding', the paper-back throw-away attitude to an article traditionally destined to be preserved. For all too long the commercial cased book work and stationery binding with its 'piece' work or bonus capability commanded higher financial rewards than the much slower craft binding. It has all added to the problem.

2.3 Library problems

In the larger, old-established libraries, which strictly speaking should only reflect a difference of degree in the conservation situation, the cumulative neglect of preservation measures created near crisis conditions. What was perfectly adequate in earlier times constituted a major conservation problem in the conditions already described. The very fact that stock had survived centuries without any real conservation attention led to a false sense of security, that it would continue to survive without any interference. Even in times of economic constraint current acquisitions in older libraries can eat up more shelf space in one year than decades accounted for in earlier centuries with all the consequent pressures on space. It is in their nature that such libraries count many rarities in their stock. The demand on these and on all rare book collections, large and small, was almost a new dimension in library use: they were no longer the sole province of the occasional scholar.

2.4 Symptoms

There have been many other less obvious factors in stimulating awareness. For example, requests from developing countries to place staff in binderies and conservation laboratories for purposes of work experience, received in growing numbers by the British Council, could not easily be met in recent years. Those institutions with appropriate facilities came under very considerable pressure. Moreover, libraries with sizeable in-house binderies, which had high standards of traditional binding but little knowledge of, or involvement in, modern conservation techniques, found such placements generally difficult to accommodate, disadvantageous to their own work and even disheartening. The result was to highlight not simply the very special problems facing Third World, tropical countries, but in particular the meagre facilities available in the UK and, for that matter, in Western countries generally. It underlined our own deficiencies and their international dimensions. British libraries, certainly, were unable to discharge what many would regard as a prime responsibility to underdeveloped countries, to provide work and training experience essential to meeting their problems. In a similar, indirect way microform promotion contributed also to the growth in awareness. A means of gaining access to inaccessible materials and the gradual development of such media as instruments of publication led to their recognition by libraries as agents of conservation. What was good for newspapers was also good for other categories of material. Some stock simply had to be protected from reader use and here was an instrument with which to achieve it.

2.5 Awareness

These were some of the background factors contributing to the growing awareness of conservation requirements. More immediate to the project was an account given by the Head of Conservation[9] in the Reference Division of the British Library to the Division's Advisory Committee in 1978 on conservation needs in the British Library. This stimulated such discussion as to encourage a member of the Committee[10] to produce a paper on the conservation needs of libraries in general, on staff awareness and policies. At the same time the pressures from overseas visitors and from those awakening to the need in the UK, on the India Office Library, the Public Record Office and others with specific conservation facilities, had become acute. The British Library Research and Development Department was urged to examine training provision in conservation and an *ad hoc* committee was formed in 1980, which recommended that the present project, or one like it, be mounted and based in a large library with conservation facilities and interests.

In that year the Cambridge Conservation Conference was held and, also at an international level, the Conference of National Libraries chose conservation as the theme of its annual meeting. The latter conference requested the National Library of Canada to undertake a survey 'of national libraries to find out what role national libraries play in national conservation activities in their country as well as the extent of their internal conservation programs'. All at once, it seemed, conservation had become a main theme in all libraries. Hitherto, libraries had seemed unconcerned to promote conservation, even at the basic essential level, let alone as a major area of library activity and, therefore, of recurrent expenditure. Even in the best-equipped and endowed libraries, conservation when compared with the expenditure on the applications of the new technology or on acquisition had been a poor relation. Perhaps the very fact that it had always been there in libraries inured them to the necessities.

3 Objectives

3.1 Formulation of objectives

The objectives of the project were set out in an announcement in the April 1982 issue of *British Library News*. From the outset it was clear that conservation could not be viewed in isolation, as some sort of appendix to established library practices and policies. On the contrary, it pointed to contact with all aspects of library life and, given an appropriate measure of priority, constituted a crucially important area of a library's administration. The objectives were refined during early meetings of the Project Committee and also extended to afford an international comparison. However, the publication in April 1982 of the survey carried out by the National Library of Canada[11] removed the need for immediate direct action within the project. Its findings are highly relevant and, with the permission of the National Libraries Conference, are utilised in this report.

The objectives of the project are to:

(1) describe and assess the conservation needs and policies of libraries in the United Kingdom;

(2) survey existing conservation provision and to prepare a 'state of the art' report on the conservation of library materials, taking into account modern developments in conservation in the context of the traditional library concept of binding;

(3) investigate and describe existing possibilities for the training of library and technical staff in conservation (including in-house training schemes and training with specific scientific content) and to indicate any gaps in provision;

(4) attempt a preliminary survey of the facilities and manpower available for specific conservation work in the United Kingdom (i.e. as opposed to binding) and indicate future needs;

(5) consider the need to establish or identify a national centre for scientific conservation investigation and for consultation;

(6) prepare advice for libraries on a strategy to be adopted in regard to the conservation of library material and to make recommendations for the immediate future;

(7) assess generally conservation provision and policies in Western countries for comparative purposes.

These objectives require no further comment except to emphasise the complicated nature of the undertaking. This created many problems even at the very early stage of the enquiry. Familiarity with the subject disguised some fundamental deficiencies in knowledge, even terminology was far from consistent. It is primarily to eliminate any uncertainty on this score that a glossary of terms used has been appended. In this and other respects this report is concerned with a number of basic issues.

3.2 Limitations

The non-technical nature of the project has already been noted: it was a limitation inherent in a work concerned primarily with the conservation attitudes, management and policies of librarians. Specific guide-lines as to the kind or level of conservation knowledge necessary for librarians are, therefore, excluded from the objectives and detailed discussion of such practical issues does not feature in the report. Nevertheless, the need for this kind of guidance has been expressed both in returns to questionnaires and at a seminar held in Cambridge, September 1983, to discuss the project[12]. It could take the shape of a 'conservation primer' for librarians comprising basic rules on what to do and what not to do. Such a publication could form the basis of any in-house training programme and should perhaps be considered as a matter of urgency, outside this report. Until then, the paper delivered at the Cambridge seminar by conservator Dr Pickwoad should go some way to meet this need and is accordingly included in the annexes to the report.

4 Method

4.1 Experience

Such broadly stated objectives could only be met by approaching a wide variety of libraries. It was essential that a Project Steering Committee be established with as broad a representation as possible within the limits of an effective committee. It represents, in addition to libraries generally, the British Library, the Library Association, the Standing Conference of National and University Libraries (SCONUL), Record Offices, the University Grants Committee, the Committee of Vice-Chancellors and Principals, the Institute of Paper Conservation and the book trade. Cambridge University Library became the host library for a number of reasons, chief among them being that it has a conservation department, a bindery and its share of problems, thus meeting the requirements specified by the *ad hoc* committee which preceded the project itself. It also has an Archives Department which acts both as a regional and university repository, so that professional archival expertise is on hand, as well as that traditionally found in Departments of Manuscripts and Printed Books. In addition it has a special kind of relevant experience in that the conservation over the last ten years of its collection of the Cairo Genizah Fragments[13], c. 140,000 in all dating from the 10th to 19th centuries AD, had established a specialist level of expertise in an area of conservation which the Library had largely pioneered. It is also at the centre of a network of college, faculty and departmental libraries which in their immense variety exhibited every condition in the conservation gamut. The Project Steering Committee, meeting on a monthly basis, was in close contact with the Project Director and the Research Assistant, acting as a sounding board and a prime research resource throughout the project.

4.2 Contacts

It was clear that, however irksome to the recipient these may be, questionnaires backed where possible with interviews and personal contacts offered the only feasible means of securing the desirable range and level of involvement. It was equally clear that as much of the existing conservation information as possible should be examined preparatory to embarking on the questionnaire approach. Apart from searching the literature, the research itself fell into three phases: a preparatory survey of the practices and policies which already exist in the archival field; a pilot questionnaire aimed at representative institutions and the main questionnaires.

It was important to secure a high level of publicity for the project, and to capitalise on the high level of concern already widespread. Apart from the British Library press release, the *Bookseller*, *Times Higher Educational Supplement*, the *Library Association Record*, *The Book Collector* and other specialist publications carried information on the project and the considerable interest in the project from outside the Committee has been maintained. Within librarianship, conservation had become a main theme in SCONUL and the start of the project was followed by the establishment of a sub-committee on conservation by the Library Association. The Crafts Council and Aslib were among the many bodies which have responded to the project team. Among the earliest reactions to the announcement of the project were letters from Australia, Canada and the USA, indicating the international interest which the project aroused.

4.3 Preliminary survey

The preparatory work took the form of a series of visits by the Research Assistant to institutions with a strong archival base, in effect a preliminary survey aimed at assessing their policies and practices so that some basis of comparison with libraries could be established. It has long been recognised that libraries and archives differ fundamentally in their approach to and concern for conservation and this is reflected in their budget, staffing, equipment and facilities. The opportunity to study long-established conservation practices in a profession so closely allied to librarianship was highly desirable and in the event proved to be crucial in the subsequent formulation of the questions. Six institutions agreed to take part in this preliminary investigation and were visited, namely, Churchill College, Cambridge, the House of Lords Record Office, Lambeth Palace Library, the Mercers' Company, the Royal Greenwich Observatory and Stationers' Hall. Four of the six had an in-house conservation workshop.

Discussions with the archivists and their conservators served to highlight the problems posed by such factors as size and nature of collections, volume of use, type of accommodation housing collections, funds available for additional storage, the different methods of conservation in use, and, perhaps most valuable of all, the ordering of priorities and the place of conservation within them. It confirmed at once, if confirmation were necessary, the great contrast in approach to conservation by archivists and librarians. Of special interest here were the different attitudes to conservation in those institutions which housed both archives and libraries. This reflected much the same picture as that distinguishing archives from libraries when in separate institutions. For a variety of reasons the archives made extensive use of the conservation workshops whilst libraries rarely had recourse to them.

The welcome given to the project by these six institutions was warmly encouraging. It exemplified the interest shown generally by those working in archives. The press release marking the beginning of the project was referred to by the *Archive Conservationists News Sheet*[14] and it was publicised by the Society of Archivists. This was to be expected from the body which opens its Annual Instructional Meeting for Archive Conservationists regularly to librarians, offering possibly the only regular opportunity for staff in libraries to discuss conservation. The project aims to complement the work already published in the field of conservation by archivists and should supplement, from a library stand-point, the valuable publication *Training in conservation* issued by the United Kingdom Institute of Conservation.

It will be evident that in addition to digesting as much of the published information as possible, the project had to tap all existing expertise. Representation from the Public Record Office on the Committee was especially useful in this respect and coupled with the close cooperation and experience gained from the six institutions already mentioned, provided a sound background of archival practice to the project team. Nowhere was this more valuable than in the compilation of a pilot questionnaire on which the subsequent enquiries were to be based.

4.4 Pilot questionnaire

The immediate priority following the preliminary work with archivists and conservators was to establish a control group, made up mostly of libraries around which the main questionnaires were to be designed. It was plain that the project would have two quite distinct aspects and that two questionnaires would be necessary for the two constituencies within the profession, namely, the practitioners and the educators. Whilst it would be invidious to attach a greater degree of importance to one or the other there was no doubt that the survey of the libraries would be a much heavier and lengthier undertaking. The main thrust of the pilot questionnaire was, therefore, directed to the actual conservation practices and policies in libraries, not at education or training. Since the final questionnaire would take the form essentially of a census questionnaire (as opposed to random sampling) it was important to ensure that the balance of libraries within the pilot questionnaire was right and properly representative. Forty-four institutions were selected: 21 university libraries, nine public libraries, one national library, nine record offices and four other institutional libraries. The emphasis on academic libraries at this stage reflected a belief that these would by their nature have the higher proportion of material to preserve. The record offices were included to verify the findings of the preliminary survey of the six archives and in particular to assess the validity of the questions. In doing so, it was accepted in principle by the Advisory Committee that record offices and archives would probably be excluded from the final questionnaires in view of the high level of awareness and provision indicated by the preliminary survey. It was evident at this early stage that this was of a totally different order to that found in libraries. The pilot questionnaire confirmed these findings.

There were four main purposes of the pilot questionnaire. The first was to test the response, the rate of completion and return. The second was to outline the types of conservation problems and needs facing the different types of institution, within the limits of questions. Thirdly, by monitoring the response to each set of questions, the scope and content of the questions for the census questionnaires were to be determined. Finally, there was a search for some statistical confirmation of the trends which earlier reports produced by members of the Committee had indicated. It was a completely exploratory exercise aimed entirely at getting the subsequent questionnaires right.

It is not proposed to deal in any detail with the pilot questionnaire. The response to it was high. Thirty-seven of the 44 institutions replied, an 84% return, which in itself was indicative of the interest aroused. Despite the small sample the results were not without interest. Ninety-five per cent of those replying agreed to follow-up interviews; 90% were in favour of a self-financing national centre to advise on conservation and to conduct research; 19% only reported any form of in-house training. The reactions within the various categories of library were mostly but not always predictable: 75% of university and public libraries were dissatisfied with training received by newly recruited qualified staff, but only 25% of record offices were; 75% of record offices and 50% of university libraries had some recourse to existing scientific expertise, whereas only 15% of public libraries did. Twenty-five per cent of university libraries had some sort of written conservation policy, 100% of public libraries had none at all.

4.5 Main questionnaire

The pilot questionnaire largely determined, therefore, the final form of the main questionnaires. It introduced significant changes in the lay-out, removed a number of ambiguities of phraseology and improved the possibilities of statistical comparison. Moreover, it enabled the whole of each questionnaire to be encompassed on one sheet of paper. Excluding those institutions already incorporated within the pilot questionnaire, the library questionnaire was despatched to 387 libraries, made up as follows: 175 public libraries; 46 government department and similar libraries; 31 polytechnic libraries; 30 university libraries; three national libraries; 27

London University college libraries; 41 Oxford University college libraries and 34 Cambridge University college libraries. The inclusion of college libraries from Oxford and Cambridge universities reflects the acknowledged importance of their holdings within the national heritage. At the same time it was recognised that these could distort the final questionnaire returns significantly since their nature and staffing are so frequently different from those of other libraries. The college libraries of the University of London are on the other hand very much libraries of the University of London, much more orthodox in their staffing and practices. The government department and miscellaneous libraries are the only groups where a selection of libraries was made so that these reflect not a census but a random approach. The numbers are so few, however, that this does not distort the findings as a whole, but to be sure the two groups are cited separately. The final total of 418 libraries approached includes 31 of the 44 institutions participating in the pilot questionnaire.

The decision to exclude record offices and archives from the final questionnaire and therefore by implication from the report was, as indicated above, assumed on completion of the preliminary survey and confirmed by the pilot questionnaire's findings. Not only were conservation practices and policies much healthier in archives when compared with libraries but it was recognised also that like was not being compared with like, that their needs were similar but not the same as those in libraries, that no parallel for the principal problem in libraries, the preservation on a huge scale of printed materials originating in all parts of the world, was to be found. It was also accepted by the Advisory Committee that libraries within museums, or similar institutions, where conservation facilities might be highly developed, albeit for other immediate purposes, should in general be excluded. The possibilities of ambiguous returns in the case of those libraries were seen to be high. As it was, despite the many improvements made on the basis of the pilot questionnaire, the returns demonstrated that the final form still offered much possibility for ambiguity to the respondents.

The education/training questionnaire was distributed to 275 institutions which it was supposed might offer training courses, whether of a practical kind for binders or conservators or of a professional kind for librarians. The main and obvious difference between the two main questionnaires was that, whereas all the libraries approached could be sure to have some involvement in conservation, of the educational institutions approached only the schools of librarianship could be said with certainty to have an interest in making provision for libraries. This exercise was, therefore, much more one of basic exploration than the other. The total included 250 colleges of technology, art and higher education, nine universities, nine polytechnics and seven other colleges. Eighteen schools of librarianship were among those approached.

The rate of response to this questionnaire has again been high. The possibility of ambiguity here is much less likely for the majority of respondents because a negative reply to the third question is virtually a negative reply to the whole questionnaire. Even so, for those institutions filling out the whole, there were again some problems of ambiguity, but, as with the questionnaire to libraries, these were not of such an order as to invalidate the findings in any way. A copy of both questionnaires is included as an appendix to the report. The use of a computer for analysing the findings made a very wide variety of cross-tabulations possible.

5 Questionnaire to libraries: findings and discussion

5.1 The returns

Of the 418 libraries approached 332 filled in and returned the questionnaire; in addition, several of the remainder returned it blank but with a covering explanatory letter. The returns contained a considerable amount of detailed information, much of it unexpected. There was also much comment of general interest which cannot be incorporated in this report, but which may well be published later.

The questionnaire bears out a great deal of the information conveyed by the pilot questionnaire. The high rate of response, 79.4% – over 80% if the explanatory letters are included – is again indicative of the level of interest or concern. Although this is slightly lower than the 84% return for the pilot questionnaire, the relatively short time available for the completion and the much larger number of libraries approached suggests a more significant success rate. The amount of information provided gratuitously by a high proportion of the respondents not only confirms the high level of interest in conservation but also conveys a sense of urgency about the need for positive action. The numerous insights into the situation conveyed by the cross-tabulations facilitated by computer entry cannot be fully utilised here. However, they are of such interest that like much of the detail supplied they may well be made available at a later date. They will in any event be retained, for future reference, in Cambridge University Library.

The findings are presented now in the order in which the questions appear on the questionnaire, with little or no comment. The first question identifying institutions is, of course, excluded from this procedure. The final request, asking signatories to indicate their position in their library, sought to ensure that the appropriate person had filled in the questionnaires and in general appears to have succeeded in that aim. Where questions have not been answered by libraries and it is not possible to deduce from the question the significance of this omission, the omission is signified by the reduced total of libraries recorded. The libraries noted in brackets, apart from the miscellaneous and government libraries, do not necessarily comprise the total number but draw attention to specific categories of library within the total. Brief discussion of the findings follows their presentation.

5.2 The findings

Question 2 29 libraries (including government, miscellaneous, 9) described their use as 'light'. The remainder fell evenly into 'medium' use (143, including government, miscellaneous, 19) and 'heavy' (139, including government, miscellaneous, 8). The fact that at least half of the 29 are essentially 'private' libraries confirms that use is a highly relevant factor in conservation today.

Question 3 Proportion of stock intended for permanent retention.

	less than 20%	21-60%	61-80%	81-100%
Libraries	68	31	17	162
(including government, miscellaneous)	(5)	(4)	(3)	(21)

Of these respondents 77 aim to retain all stock (including 28 public, 13 university, 2 polytechnic, 2 national, 10 government, miscellaneous); 35 university and 45 public libraries will retain over 80% of their holdings; 38 will retain less than 10% (including 1 university, 7 polytechnic, 29 public); 1 university library proposes to retain none at all permanently.

Question 4 Written policy statement.
Only 4 university, 2 public, 2 government and 1 national library have a written policy statement.

Question 5 (a) 50 libraries have an in-house bindery (including 22 university, 19 public, all national, 3 government, miscellaneous).
(b) 26 libraries have a conservation workshop (including 9 university, 9 public, all national, 3 miscellaneous).
(c) 86 libraries have repair facilities of some kind (including 15 university, 36 public, 7 polytechnic, 7 government, miscellaneous).
(d) 144 libraries have access to facilities elsewhere (including 18 university, 60 public, 1 national, 5 polytechnic, 11 Cambridge colleges, 20 Oxford colleges, 9 London colleges, 20 government, miscellaneous).

Question 6 (a) 198 libraries make use of outside firms for all specialist

repair work (including 24 government, miscellaneous).
62 libraries make use of outside firms for some specialist repair work (including 7 government, miscellaneous).
(b) 260 libraries make use of outside firms for all standard bindings (including 28 government, miscellaneous).
41 libraries make use of outside firms for some standard binding (including 5 government, miscellaneous).

Question 7 (a) 61 libraries employ binders (including 22 public, 24 university, 3 national, 4 government, miscellaneous).
39 libraries employ 5 binders or under (86 binders between them).
22 libraries employ 6 binders or over (343 binders between them).
(b) 30 libraries employ conservation technicians.

Question 8 (a) 143 libraries have a member of staff responsible for ordering conservation priorities (including 63 public, 28 university, 7 polytechnic, all national, 15 government, miscellaneous).
(b) 165 libraries have a member of staff specifying repairs on individual items (including 70 public, 34 university, 7 polytechnic, all national, 21 government, miscellaneous).

Question 9 (a) The following factors in environmental control are taken into account by the number of libraries as shown: temperature 125, humidity 102, storage conditions 42, lighting 35, security 29, pollution/dust control 25, use 19.
(b) 178 libraries (including 24 government, miscellaneous) cannot adjust air-conditioning, humidity, etc.
36 libraries (including 3 government, miscellaneous) can adjust air-conditioning, humidity, etc.
106 libraries (including 10 government, miscellaneous) have some partial control.
(c) 173 libraries do not monitor stack/repository conditions, 127 do, 7 do in part.
(d) *Temperature*[15] *ranges reported (°F)*

Minimum to maximum	Libraries	including government, miscellaneous
45-54	6	1
55-64	59	7
65-74	80	7
75-84	1	0

171 libraries were unable to provide reliable information.

Relative humidity[15] *ranges reported (%)*

Minimum to maximum	Libraries	including government, miscellaneous
Below 40	3	2
40-49	3	0
50-59	47	7
60-69	33	5
70-79	2	0
Above 80	2	0

(e) 154 libraries have no systematic procedure for surveying or treating stock on the shelves, 126 do have a procedure. Of those having surveys and treating stock 32 carry them out annually and 67 frequently (weekly in some cases), 25 'infrequently'.

The types of treatment prescribed from such surveys include repair 60, leather dressing 46, furbishing 28, fumigation 5, lamination 6, replacement 4, deacidification 6, encapsulation 1, reboxing 6 and 'rebinding' 56 (presumably despatched for rebinding).

Question 10 189 libraries (including 27 government, miscellaneous) report newly qualified staff receiving no training in conservation, 65 libraries (including 5 government, miscellaneous) a minimal amount, 26 libraries (including 1 government, miscellaneous) basic training of some kind.

Question 11 282 have no in-house programme in preservation awareness, 36 do have (including 15 public, 11 university, 3 national, 3 miscellaneous).

Question 12 159 libraries do have recourse to existing scientific expertise, 166 (including government, miscellaneous 19) do not. Of those which do, 64 make use of university departments, 47 of museums, 42 of conservation laboratories, 20 of industrial concerns and 55 of other facilities.

Question 13 55 libraries subscribe to conservation journals specifically, 249 do not.

Question 14 (a) and (b) Return cannot be cited because of the individual nature of returns; they confirm 14(c).
(c) 243 libraries spend a sum equivalent to 0-29% of their acquisition budget on conservation, 11 the

	equivalent of 30-59%, 2 from 60-89%, 2 over 90%, 3 the equivalent of 100%.
Question 15	(a) 196 use microforms as a means of preservation, 128 do not. Their main use is in the conservation of newspapers, then manuscripts, periodicals and rarities in descending order. (b) 254 have no microfilm production facilities, 69 do. (c) 220 have no special storage area for microforms, 96 do.
Question 16	(a) 173 libraries think there is a need for a national centre, 79 think not, 25 do not know. (b) 107 libraries would use such a centre, 152 would not, 24 do not know.
Question 17	19 libraries indicated experiencing difficulties in obtaining specific products for use in conservation repair.
Question 18	121 libraries instruct users in the handling of books, 199 do not.
Question 19	104 libraries offered further comment on conservation. The most common observations related to finance, i.e. inadequate finance to meet the necessary conservation requirements.
Question 20	222 libraries, about 66% of the participating libraries, agreed to be interviewed by the Research Assistant.

5.3 Discussion

As was expected, the returns confirm much that has been hitherto assumed or suspected but they also contain some surprises. The fact that only 9% of the libraries described their level of use as 'light', the remainder being 'heavy' or 'medium', must identify use as a crucial piece in the preservation picture (Q. 2). Though this return must be to some extent subjective, few librarians would doubt its accuracy. The growth in library use is one of the post-war facts of library life and the consequent 'wear and tear' on stock is central to the conservation problem. Much more surprising and in their implications more difficult to accept are the returns relating to retention of stock. The number of libraries intending to keep over 80% of their stock permanently is much higher than was expected (Q. 3). The fact that 28 public, 13 university and two polytechnic libraries aim to retain all their stock permanently in addition to the national libraries puts the national archive of printed materials into a new perspective. No less surprising here is that 29 public, seven polytechnic and one university library expect to hold little or no stock on a permanent basis. Retention of stock must be at the heart of any preservation problem. How realistic it is for 77 libraries to aim at the wholesale retention of stock raises the whole question of national policies. The fact that 162 will retain 81-100% underlines the need for a realistic national plan.

The few libraries with written policy statements (Q. 4), nine in all, come as no surprise: the practice of written policy statements generally is still predominantly an American rather than a British library exercise. The number of in-house binderies (Q. 5) must reflect the tendency in the post-war period to incorporate binderies in new library buildings, certainly as far as university libraries are concerned. The in-house conservation workshop, however, is a much more recent development as awareness has grown. Together, given the numbers of libraries proposing to retain large quantities of stock permanently, the provision is hardly extensive. Taken in conjunction with the returns to question 7, which show 39 libraries employing five binders or fewer, the generally low level of provision within institutions becomes apparent. The total number of binders working within the 61 libraries employing such staff amounts to 429, of conservation technicians within the 30 libraries involved to 93. Of these the British Library contributed 150 and 20 respectively. The returns to questions 5(c) and (d), and 6(a) and (b) are largely predictable; they are nonetheless of special interest in confirming the continuing onus which is placed on the trade bindery. The majority of libraries still entrust their conservation work to binders and conservators outside the institution to which the stock belongs with all the implications which such a practice holds for consultation and liaison between library and binders. This raises another fundamental issue within library conservation policies. The replies to question 8 suggest, on a more detailed analysis than can be presented here, that in general a low level of professional involvement and responsibility obtains in what is a conservation key position. It points to a somewhat diffident approach to conservation in the overall priorities of libraries.

The returns to question 9 go to the core of another of the main problems of conservation. Even where specific factors in environmental control are identified by libraries, few can really exercise control in any absolute sense. Given that most of the libraries record heavy or medium use, very few (19) cited use as a factor in preservation. Whilst financial considerations, both capital and recurrent expenditure, must loom large in most environmental controls, these are aspects which lie within a library's individual policies and depend essentially on the ordering of priorities. It is disquieting to learn that only a minority of libraries have systematic procedures for surveying stock or monitoring stack and open-shelf conditions. The extraordinary ranges in temperature and humidity reported by some libraries must be a cause for anxiety. As regards the six libraries operating in extremely low ranges (45-54 °F), it would be interesting to learn how their stock fares. Though highly unsatisfactory for staff, indeed illegal in terms of the Factory Act[16], such temperatures are eminently suitable for the preservation of stock. Comments in the returns on environmental controls include: 'Nothing special. The library is heated to suit the needs of the readers', 'We have no control over the library environment (even to preserve our physical comfort)', 'We can open windows'. What unfortunately cannot be deduced from the returns is the impact, within libraries designed to operate with air-conditioning, when plants fail. Loss of such technical services for any length of time may well lay up problems for the future. Two incidents in Cambridge University Library will illustrate this. In a recent university economy drive, the Head of Library Technical Services switched off air-conditioning in the stacks daily for 12 hours when the building was closed without consulting other staff. It resulted in the saving of much electricity but also led to a widespread outbreak of fungal growth with cost implications far exceeding those made from the savings of electricity. Again, during the recent very hot summer, the air-conditioning plant broke down for a fortnight. Temperatures in the rare-books stacks quickly rose to 100 °F with no alternative means of reducing them until the plant was repaired. The questionnaire cannot supply this kind of information.

Questions 10 and 11 provide information which complements that revealed by the training questionnaire. Effectively, newly qualified staff have received no training in conservation on recruitment to libraries, since even the 'minimal' amounts referred to by the respondents rarely amount to more than the occasional lecture or class. The virtual absence of in-house instruction in conservation means that the age-old method of learning from experience and from example remains the chief source of preservation knowledge. Against a background of neglect or low priority this is hardly encouraging. It is of little value to staff except in the very long term and it is decidedly bad for the books. There is little of immediate practical value in the literature to assist library staff, at least of the basic kind needed. The further fact (Q. 13) that only one-sixth of the libraries subscribe to conservation journals of any kind may be taken as additional evidence of general educational deficiencies, but it underlines also the difficult position in which library staff find themselves.

The comparatively high number of libraries claiming to make use of existing scientific expertise (Q. 12) is encouraging on the face of it but must be limited in the light of their budgets. Of interest here is the relatively slight use made of the industrial centres outside public institutions. This must certainly be due in part to the fact that use of such centres would probably incur expenditure, whereas institutional aid may well be without charge for many libraries. The returns to 14(a) and (b) are difficult to present but they confirm categorically the minimal levels of expenditure indicated by 14(c). Many libraries have great difficulty in arriving at any clear idea of the overall costs. With regard to microforms (Q. 15(a)), the main use by the 196 libraries is to limit newspaper handling whilst for many the acquisition of microforms is a substitute for purchase of the normal format. The answers to 15(b) support this but, more significantly, along with the returns to 15(c), they reveal a high incidence of inadequate provision of basic library photographic requirements. The inadvisability of storing silver halide and diazo film together is still largely ignored in many libraries.

The answers to question 16(a), especially when related to those to question 12, endorse the emphatic opinion expressed in the pilot questionnaire that there is a real need for a national centre. The replies to 16(b), however, whilst encouraging in that 107 would use such a centre, are possibly more important for the statement from 152 libraries that they would not be prepared to pay for its services. This must be taken to mean that they would be unable to pay and it brings one of the main issues in conservation, available finance, right to the fore. Some 50 of the participating libraries did not answer either part of 16, so presumably also belong to the 'don't knows'. The details of the positive returns are not without interest.

16. (a) *Need for a national centre*

			Prepared to pay for services	
	Yes	No	Yes	No
Cambridge colleges	7	6	4	10
Government libraries	5	3	4	6
London University colleges	12	7	7	15
Miscellaneous	12	6	9	10
National libraries	2	1	2	0
Oxford colleges	16	6	5	20
Polytechnic libraries	13	8	7	15
Public libraries	71	38	43	61
University libraries	35	4	26	15
	173	79	107	152

The answers to question 17 seem to run counter to views expressed in the Project Committee. Concern there about availability of materials was such that a sub-committee to investigate cooperative purchasing in bulk was convened and will probably continue after the project has been completed. This concern was also echoed at the Cambridge seminar. The large number of libraries not answering the question may indicate simply that the staff did not know, which would be highly likely where conservation was carried out by external firms or where the level of conservation awareness is low. It could also mean, unfortunately, that unsuitable but available materials were being used and accepted by libraries unaware of the problems which would arise. The returns suggest that large libraries, with in-house facilities, such as those represented on the sub-committee, will find cooperative purchasing of real value (two national, seven public and five university libraries are among the 19 respondents). Question 18 produced a response which was also surprising in view of the absence of in-house instruction for library staff. No less than half (60) of those advising readers were public libraries. The instruction may only be at a rudimentary level but it is an important step in promoting conservation consciousness and library staff must be involved. Questions 19 and 20 provided responses of general significance. The very fact that 104 libraries offered further comment on a variety of themes and that 222 agreed to be interviewed by the Research Assistant if time allowed demonstrated again the real level of concern which is now current.

Perhaps a further comment of a general kind should be made at this point. Whilst the responses to the individual questions are important in themselves they cannot convey the sense of unease which a perusal of all the individual returns induces. Collectively they create an impression which amounts to unsolicited evidence of the educational need and the low priority traditionally attached to conservation which is difficult to quantify. It is akin to the dismay which some librarians feel when witnessing the handling of materials by readers on self-service photocopying machines so frequently found in libraries today.

6 Questionnaire on training: findings and discussion

6.1 The returns

Of the 275 questionnaires despatched, 234 were returned, an 85% response. This apparently high success rate contained, however, only 32 positive replies, that is replies indicating that conservation of some kind was part of the curriculum of the institution. Since the questionnaire was concerned to discover educational opportunities available and, therefore, the extent of training received not just by librarians, but by binders and conservators also, the significance of the 32 returns is reduced even further. Only 13.6% of the 234 institutions replying include conservation in their curricula. If it were to be concluded that the 41 institutions not returning the questionnaires abstained because conservation did not feature in their curricula at all, a not unreasonable assumption, the proportion of institutions offering courses of some kind falls to 11.5%.

The small number of positive replies constitutes in itself perhaps the most important information elucidated by the questionnaire. The high incidence of blank spaces among the returns, when compared with the other main questionnaire, also suggests that even where the response is positive, conservation is of rather less than consuming interest in higher and further education. Moreover, a number of respondents indicate that the course was aimed at the general public rather than at the professionally motivated, circumscribing yet again the professional opportunities which might be inferred from the returns. Having said that, it was reported that several of the evening classes of this kind frequently find librarians and archivists among their students.

6.2 The findings and discussion

Given the few positive returns, presentation in the manner of the preceding questionnaire is hardly possible. The individual and varied nature of the replies also speaks against it. It is proposed, therefore, to discuss the findings in a more general way emphasising points of special interest. The responses came from the following types of institutions: 16 colleges of higher education, art and technology; six universities; four polytechnics;

three colleges of art and three other institutions. Eleven of the replies came from schools of librarianship (five in universities, four in polytechnics and two in colleges): seven library schools did not return the questionnaire. Of the 29 institutions providing courses in conservation (Q. 3), 10 indicated that they constituted courses in themselves, 19 that they were part of other courses. In the remaining three the content was insufficient to describe it in terms of a course. Fourteen of the courses were aimed at librarians (Q. 4), nine at binders and eight at conservation technicians, but with much content common to each course, and 13 of the courses are described as being of general interest to the public. Seven courses (Q. 6) were for undergraduates, that is part of an undergraduate course, and five were part of postgraduate library school courses. The other full-time (14), part-time (14), day release (five) and evening (eight) courses were essentially for binders, conservators and the general public. There is considerable overlap in objectives and interest among the non-graduate courses.

The responses to questions 7 to 10 reflect the widely varying possibilities among courses, whether aimed at librarians, conservators or binders. Duration of courses, for example (Q. 7), ranges from four hours to four years part-time. The full-time courses for undergraduates at library schools refer undoubtedly to the whole undergraduate course and contain a relatively minor element for conservation. Normal entrance requirements (Q. 8) can only be viewed in relation to individual courses, some for binding having no requirements whilst those for degree and postgraduate courses reflect standard university entry procedures. The same kind of observation applies to question 9 where maximum numbers can be as high as 40 but where in local education institutions the main concern is to identify the minimum number on which a course can run. Question 10 is valuable for the way in which it identifies conservation as part of some other activity, such as historical bibliography, paper-making or binding techniques. Frequently conservation plays a very limited part in such general courses and contact with conservators as such is rare.

Not unexpectedly, question 11 shows that library schools dwelt heavily on their courses on management and administration whilst courses for binding and conservation concentrated on the technical and scientific background. The latter were those most likely to invite visiting lecturers to talk on their speciality. The scientific content reported in the returns is in general far removed from the advanced scientific work discussed in the conservation science literature and where it occurs is of a basic background nature. For obvious reasons the binders and conservators should be much better served in their courses, in theory at least, than are librarians since conservation can only be part of the curricula of library schools. Moreover, it has long been possible to acquire City and Guilds qualifications in binding so that whatever their standard the curricula are firmly developed. Conservation for librarians is very likely to be a new element in usually crowded curricula whether at diploma, undergraduate or postgraduate level. Practical work (Q. 12) tends to occur only in courses for binders and conservators, but most students (Q. 13) encounter original materials at some time, however briefly.

Questions 14 to 17 reflect the policies of the institution mounting the courses. The most significant return of these four is that to question 16, which suggests that the number of individuals involved in teaching courses corresponds to the number of institutions returning positive questionnaires. The most frequent observation in reply to question 17 was that the inculcation of awareness of conservation need and techniques was the main objective. Four suggested (Q. 18) that there should be higher degrees in binding and conservation whilst others thought there was a need for degrees in specialist fields such as paper conservation and craft binding. Whilst degree courses are possible in this field and, indeed, are being introduced in the USA, it is difficult to envisage the content of degree courses in the UK, at least, for potential members of staff in libraries.

6.3 Training courses

There are other considerations in the returns which again limit rather than enhance the available facilities. Many of the courses in the colleges, though open to librarians, do not have library interests specifically in mind. They are, for example, likely to be aimed as much at the production of leather technologists or museum technicians as they are at the training of binders and conservators. Again, as already indicated, several of the part-time courses concerned with book-binding are offered very much as a recreation activity with no qualifications involved. These are bound to be structured differently from those part-time courses directed specifically at educating binders and conservation technicians, which do carry a final qualification. Even among the full-time courses there can be great variations in content. For example, scientific content is variously described in five of these courses as 'nil' (1), '10-30% of course' (3), 'strong emphasis on science throughout' (1).

In most of the library school courses the scientific content varies from negligible to non-existent. After management and administration, they touch collectively on such issues as the need for conservation, environmental considerations, conservation techniques, special collection management, rare book librarianship, archival repairs, physical bibliography and such like. Most of the respondents agree that their attention to conservation is at a basic introductory level. As one commented: 'This field is an obvious candidate for inclusion in curriculum development in the near future'. One early reaction to the training questionnaire was a number of proposals from library schools to start courses in conservation or to enhance the present rather basic approach.

Significantly, the most highly developed courses available exist outside the library field, being clearly directed towards other professions. Two such bodies, one concerned primarily with archaeology, the other with archives, incorporate conservation at a level which is immediately relevant to libraries. This must be true, also, with modest adaptation of existing courses, of university departments of Polymer and Fibre Science which were excluded from the survey. This area of scientific technology has long incorporated Paper Science as an important part of its activities and is a highly developed subject. The presence of chairs and lectureships in Paper Science suggests that specialised and relevant courses must exist quite outside the obvious and traditional library and archival disciplines. An interview with a university lecturer in one Paper Science Department confirmed that there was little or no contact with librarians in the context of teaching and research, and that they would be prepared to consider research specifically related to the conservation requirements of libraries and archives on a contract basis. Much the same may be said of PIRA (The Research Association for the Paper & Board, Printing and Packaging Industries) which is primarily concerned with industrial research requirements at a sophisticated level. The Institute of Paper Conservation and like bodies can also be visualised as having a major, much enhanced, role to play in developments of this kind.

6.4 Manpower problems

Offers to start courses in conservation in library schools and suggestions that first and higher degrees should be developed in craft binding and paper conservation, whatever their intrinsic merit, would be unlikely to provide the kind of injection into the training of librarians which libraries are looking for. Throughout the project the Committee has emphasised that in purely library professional terms the requirement is for librarians with conservation knowledge not for conservation library specialists. Few libraries will be recruiting conservators in professional library grades. They will be looking for library staff with a sound knowledge of conservation criteria. In this respect the British requirement seems very different from that which Cunha[17] described in the USA. The School of Library Service at Columbia University introduced a three-year graduate level Program for Conservators of Library and Archival Materials in 1981 and there is little doubt that such courses will spread. It underlines the different approach to the problem in the USA, but then much of the American professional library education differs from that in the UK. It seems certain that here for the foreseeable future library staff will be required primarily to discharge traditional library duties of which conservation management will be one part. The present critical situation does not call for a huge intake of specialist conservators, but for librarians in the professional grades with knowledge and awareness of conservation.

The actual process of conserving stock will continue to place heavy demands on traditional binding skills and modern conservation technology. It seems certain therefore that libraries will require increasingly the services of binders and conservation technicians to work at the bench with access to the consultant conservator. A contributory factor to the present crisis has been the great reduction in skilled craftsmen which has gradually taken place in the post-war period, particularly in the trade binderies outside institutions, with the consequent loss of training opportunities for would-be recruits to the craft. There is no substitute for the system of apprentices which was the backbone of recruitment for all types of binders providing an indispensable background for the craftsmen so essential to conservation. The establishing of in-house binderies in libraries is playing an important part in preserving one of the oldest crafts and could contribute much more by placing greater emphasis on the recruitment of the young on apprenticeship principles. Binding in Britain to-day, however, is far from being 'l'art presque oublié' referred to in *Figaro*. The scale of its continuing presence in Britain, both in institutions and in the trade, is very different too from the provision in the United States. As Stam[18] notes in his report: 'The better situation [in Britain]...has also been influenced by a strong and sound binding tradition generally unavailable in the United States'.

Conservation awareness for librarians of the future can be achieved without major new developments, through reorganisation, changes of direction in library school curricula, redevelopment of existing resources. Guaranteeing the continuing skills of the craftsmen in the appropriate numbers, which must continue to be required in the preservation of stock, will be much more difficult to achieve. The question of available skilled manpower must be to the fore in any future discussions. It brings pay, conditions of employment, status, unionism and all those other factors which have dogged the position of craftsmen in public service institutions into question. The fact, already noted, that trade cased work has for years been more remunerative than hand sewn craft binding, and never more so than in recent time, identifies the failure of librarians and others to distinguish between skills and output, between quality and quantity. It also points to failure even to recognise the difference. How else can so many rare books in libraries have come into the hands of trade binders and been indiscriminately cased or worse except through lack of scholarly appreciation and scholarly knowledge in librarians? The need to keep abreast of ever-increasing intake is no real explanation. Indeed, the pressures of acquisition, the continuing growth in the level of publication, make conservation judgment all the more important. Paradoxically, binding skills seem to have decreased in direct proportion to the increase in publication.

6.5 Preservation problems

Pressures on library staff, on shelf space and on reducing budgets are not the only problems with implications for conservation which increased acquisitions have created in libraries. Misguided conservation effort, incongruously bound or repaired books, has much to answer for in libraries today. Then there is the quality of the book itself. The oversewing or cleat-sewing of new stock is essentially an attempt to lengthen the life of 'perfect' bindings. Its use elsewhere will be prohibited by the conservationally aware librarian and discrimination is called for even with perfect bindings. The increasing evidence of such binding practices in present publications, the growth in inferior bindings, has contributed significantly to the problems on library shelves. Moreover, it makes its mark very much more quickly than acidity in paper. It has also played its part in the further down-grading of binding skills. Ironically, many such books are produced to meet the demands arising from the growth of education which has itself led to the dramatic increases in use of libraries over the last 25 years. These then are crucial factors in conservation. One of the reasons for the much more enlightened approach to conservation in archives must lie in the nature of their holdings and service, the need to protect all their materials all the time, not simply the rare or scarce, from the attention of numerous users. The need for preservation action and for the 'right' action, is overwhelmingly obvious when virtually all the materials are sensitive to use.

6.6 Short courses

It is appropriate to mention here the SCONUL Historical Bibliography and Binding courses. The latter were organised by the late Dr W S Mitchell, Librarian of the University of Newcastle upon Tyne, and comprised both general and advanced courses. They took place at intervals determined by the Conference and were usually located at Oxford. Although primarily concerned with the history of bindings, they inevitably involved the making and use of books and also generated a great deal of conservation awareness. Lectures and demonstrations by leading authorities, both from the field of bibliographical scholarship and the binding trade, stimulated a level of interest which left a permanent mark on those fortunate enough to attend. The courses were short and the attendance limited to the representation which SCONUL member librarians could afford. Many of those today in university and national libraries with an awareness of conservation needs owe this to those brief glimpses into conservation during their SCONUL courses. Such short courses with high-level input suggest a pattern for action which should accommodate even the most depressed purse.

7 Microforms and non-book media

7.1 The present situation

It was in the 19th century that John Benjamin Dancer invented microphotography on daguerreo-type plates. Microfilm and other microforms will have been with most practising librarians today for the whole of their professional lives and they would hardly include them among the 'new media'. Yet it is only in the last decade or so that microforms have made a serious impact on libraries in the UK, long after the widespread popular belief that they were destined to replace the book in its traditional format had been laid to rest. The American Research Libraries report by Reichmann and Tharpe[19] noted that in 1970 the average research library in the USA had 28 microforms for every 100 printed books. It is questionable whether that level has yet been reached in British research libraries and if it has, as was the case then in the USA, it is not in the context of preservation.

The returns to the questionnaire relating to use of microforms have been briefly referred to earlier. As far as conservation goes, they can hardly be described as positive. Of the 196 libraries claiming to use microforms as a means of conservation, only 69 at the most have microfilm production facilities, the type of microform most likely to be produced in libraries. Since the majority use relates to newspapers, there can be little doubt that this refers to purchase of microforms as a means of acquisition rather than as a deliberate policy of substitution for existing stock. On the contrary, it seems highly likely that no library in the UK, even the British Library, has yet developed a systematic microform programme for preservation purposes.

This is hardly surprising. If, as is abundantly clear from the survey, libraries have inadequate funds to undertake traditional means of conservation, they are unlikely to find within their budgets funds for conservation measures by other means. Production of microform for a master negative and security positive copy is by no means inexpensive. Where libraries do use microform at present in a conservation context, it is to meet the immediate need of a particular book not as part of a systematic microform preservation programme. The exceptions to this are the British Library Newspaper Collection at Colindale and, possibly, the Lending Division's treatment of theses, though conservation is not the prime target there. Whatever the cost of copying and the recopying often envisaged in the future, a systematic programme of microform production for preservation lies far beyond the budgets of most British libraries.

7.2 Microform conservation

Funding, important as it must be, is not the only factor to consider. It is evident from the survey that only comparatively few libraries enjoy anything like full control of their library environment. Accordingly, when 96 libraries indicate that they have a 'special storage area for microforms' the question must arise as to whether this special place has appropriate environmental controls. Much has been written about the production of microfilms for preservation purposes and why it has to be even more rigorously controlled than archival microfilming. The stability of microfilms depends very much on the maintenance of correct temperature and humidity levels. Their archival value is determined by the quality of the original filming and environmental storage conditions. If environmental controls are not generally available in a library, the conditions essential for the long-term preservation of microforms are unlikely to be present. Microforms may solve some conservation problems, but they also pose one which is peculiarly their own.

Reader access and convenience has been a major consideration in the slow progress made by microform. In the NRCd Technical Evaluation Report[20] of 1973 it states: 'All suggests that using a reader will never, and can never, be as easy as reading from the medium we are all used to: printing on paper. The various reader configurations may overcome one or some of the differences, but others will remain'. This will probably be true of all screen display presentations, microform or other technology, unless unforeseen changes come about, although a new generation of library users, conditioned to use terminals at school, may find them much more acceptable. However, reading machines bring problems other than those for the users in the shape of a variety of costs. There are the costs of the equipment, both to produce microforms and to read them, the cost of the photographic materials, of the special storage facilities and of the staff to handle them. It is in the nature of microforms that they are easily mislaid, misfiled and damaged so that apart from COM catalogues they are rarely on open access. Moreover, as long as microforms are for use within the library, not for loan, they present their own space problem in that both machines and users are a captive audience, bound to take up space within the library. Microforms may be the answer to one sort of space problem but they bring their own space requirements.

7.3 Current use

Their role in most British libraries at this time, if only on grounds of cost, would seem to extend only to the replacement of photographable but otherwise unconservable stock. As Cunha points out: 'It is probably the best answer for brittle books and newspaper collections'[21]. As far as the latter are concerned the nature and frequently the size of the materials makes microfilm an especially attractive option to the librarian although, after years of research on suitable reading machines, it still poses difficulties for the reader both in identifying issues and in the frequent necessity of reading a magnified portion of a large opening on a relatively small screen. Nevertheless, whilst it is undoubtedly much easier to use the original, it is also easier for the user to comprehend the nature of the conservation problem. The British Library Working Party on Access to Newspapers devoted much time to these problems. In many respects its work was much concerned with conservation needs.

The brittle book, as Stam noted, is less of an immediate problem in the UK, although the condition is in no way unknown. Given that heating and lighting conditions in the UK approximate more and more to those in the USA, it is merely a matter of time before books reach the stage now so widespread there. Moreover, should conservation stock surveys be undertaken, as is hoped, many more examples are likely to be revealed than are presently suspected. For the moment, however, the only possible policy seems to be the continuation of present practices, that is using microform substitutes as occasion, brittle book or otherwise, demands. The need for a National Register of Microform Masters does not have to be emphasised. The Canadian Survey of national libraries indicated that 80% of the responding libraries used microfilming as a conservation measure and that newspapers, manuscripts and periodicals were the items most commonly filmed.

7.4 National Reprographic Centre for documentation

The role of the National Reprographic Centre for documentation must be highly relevant to the growing use of microforms as a preservation agent. Library requirements, if this medium is to be used extensively, clearly presuppose a much closer liaison with the Centre. Libraries hitherto have not turned instinctively to the Centre for advice on their many photographic problems. Indeed, it was not represented on the British Library Working Party on Access to Newspapers, which as noted above devoted much time to this form of preservation activity. The LISC seminar and the Cambridge seminar brought this lack of liaison by libraries with a national body very much to the fore.

7.5 The future

Whilst a future role for microforms in preservation seems certain and easy to identify, that of other developing media can only be a matter of speculation. That they will have a role is not in doubt but it is only possible to speak in terms of their potential at present. In some respects it is difficult to see instant returns from these new technological aids given the long period taken by microforms to achieve any positive place in libraries. The archival success of these is still subject to many conditions and remains to be proved. There is a variety of unknowns in any new development. The claims as to the archival possibilities of the videodisc and optical digital disc systems must be treated with caution until substantiated by much more than existing evidence. Most librarians are still probably more aware of their vulnerability, the ease with which records can be erased, than they are of their long-term archival strengths.

In regard to the applications of such new media, experiments in the USA are directly relevant to the needs of all libraries. The investigation by the Library of Congress into video and optical disc technology and its potential for preservation is clearly of great interest. Its findings, due in 1984, must influence decisively library attitudes to these developments. It is also difficult to ignore opinion already expressed in the USA which points to an important future for such media. 'Advantages of these laser-read systems include extremely dense storage capacities, faster, more convenient retrieval and improved access because of the potential for deeper levels of indexing, virtually no wear and tear on the disc surface, and the possibility of enhancing faded or discoloured images. Whilst questions remain concerning cost, copyright, image permanence, and the impact of such a major format change on library operations, the evidence thus far indicates that video and optical disc systems offer great promise as media for processing information now in formats that are rapidly deteriorating in collections throughout the country'[22]. Given the expectations and hopes expressed over the years for microforms, the lesson with this and all new media must be to hasten slowly.

This report is not concerned with the technical processes of conservation but mass deacidification programmes are referred to elsewhere in the report and have been widely reported. *New Scientist*'s[23] account of the process developed by NASA's Goddard Space Flight Center states that the neutralisation of acid and protective alkaline treatment has 'an estimated cost of $3-5 a volume' and that 'the treatment is less expensive than microfilming, but still not cheap'. The National Library of Canada[24] quotes a similar cost of 3-4 Canadian dollars per volume for the Wei T'o mass deacidification programme currently being introduced there. Details of deacidification processes provided by eight of the 17 national libraries reporting such treatment, namely Bulgaria, Czechoslovakia, German Democratic Republic, Hungary, Italy, New Zealand, Spain, are provided in the Canadian survey but without indications of cost. Should the methods being developed prove successful, as already seems likely, it will not obviate the need to use new media but it will obviously have very considerable impact on the extent of their use.

There are many unknown quantities in regard to the use of new technology. The stability of new media, the permanence of the image, not least the implications for users, all are still very much an open question. The only fact which can be stated with absolute confidence is that, for the present certainly and for the foreseeable future most probably, they entail costs of a similar order to those which have been largely responsible for making conservation the problem it is today. The most frequent observation, common to all categories of library participating in the survey, has been that there is insufficient funding to meet essential conservation needs. Is this likely to be any different in the contemplation of conservation by the use of new media? Whatever treatment of acidic books and new media book substitutes are possible, these will avail in no way if adequate funding is not forthcoming.

8 National advisory and research centre

8.1 Need

The significant number of libraries supporting the idea of a self-financing advisory and research centre and the numbers making use of some kind of scientific expertise outside their own institution underline the need to establish a focal point for preservation affairs at national level. A variety of opinions as to what such a centre should be and do have emerged and if, collectively, they appear over-ambitious, they are none the less important indicators of the need felt by many libraries. In the main, they emphasise the consultative rather than practical potential of such a development, the collection and dissemination of information, although a few libraries looked for practical assistance too from such a centre.

The various functions most frequently stated may be summarised as to:

(1) give advice on the conservation problems of individual institutions and recommend appropriate conservation measures where possible;

(2) validate conservation materials, new equipment and machinery and advise on purchase;

(3) promote research into conservation and ensure that its results reach libraries in the form of practical guidance;

(4) assess relevant research carried out in conservation, relate it to library needs and filter the research literature;

(5) act as a conservation conference organising body;

(6) arrange training programmes for both librarians and conservators, e.g. by mounting short courses and seminars, inviting experts from the UK and abroad to participate;

(7) provide a forum for experts in library and related conservation fields;

(8) act as a communication channel for librarians and other interested parties and to publish a newsletter, journal or similar bulletin;

(9) draw up models for conservation statements as part of library policy and to advise on 'disaster planning';

(10) promote and maintain interest in preservation in the library profession, to stimulate cooperation and liaise with other professions and associations with conservation interests.

8.2 Status of the centre

Varying views were expressed by the respondents and those participating in the two seminars about the location of the centre and the form it might take. Some thought that each of the three national libraries should establish a centre, building on existing resources. Others believed that regional centres should be developed, perhaps incorporating specialist repair facilities. Another view supported Stam that a British centre 'will be best sited within the British Library Preservation Service (Reference Division)'. As already noted, this would find a precedent in the USA where the National Preservation Office is based in the Library of Congress. On the other hand, others stated that any such centre should be an independent body apart from the British Library. In this respect the Canadian survey[25] points out that the average national library 'does not provide a conservation/advisory service to other libraries in the country'.

No less mixed are the opinions as to the make-up of the centre. If, as some proposed, a centre were envisaged in terms of a building, laboratories and repair shops with all the associated staffing, a very considerable order of capital and recurrent expenditure would be required. It would be unrealistic to place much hope on that kind of establishment materialising in today's financial climate. The possibility of regional centres developing on similar lines, though undertaking preservation work on a charging basis, is equally remote even as a cooperative venture. Not only do they presuppose significant funding, but it is also difficult to see how such centres, whilst possibly meeting local service requirements, could meet the national need for documentation and dissemination of conservation research.

A body capable of discharging the various functions suggested need not necessarily be such a sizeable and expensive undertaking. A less ambitious, but effective and more easily attainable solution, would be a centre conceived in terms of a national bureau, with a purely advisory, consultative and organisational role. A complement of two research staff, preferably a chemist and librarian with conservation skills, with two clerical staff, could meet most of the requirements expressed above. The salary costs envisaged in such an establishment, including pension, insurance and the like, could be contained within about £45,000 per annum. Overhead costs would be determined by the location of such a centre. Since a separate establishment would be prohibitively high, it seems certain that it would need to be associated with another institution, either a large library or a large library school, both of which possibilities have been suggested. Were either of these possible, capital costs would be low and it should not be difficult to secure assistance from a charitable trust or even from the government. Much of the recurrent funding could be derived from a modest subscription by the many libraries which have expressed an interest (e.g. 400 libraries @ £125). There are also trade and industrial interests which may well be prepared to invest in such an undertaking. It could operate essentially as a grant-aided enterprise, of which there are several successful examples in the UK, such as the National Institute of Agricultural Botany, supported by the Ministry of Agriculture, Fisheries and Food.

8.3 Location

The location of the centre would be largely determined, after salaries and overhead costs, by such essentials as ready access to the widest range of necessary literature and regular contact with the practitioners, both conservators and binders. There are few international comparisons to which to turn for guidance. Only the USA has comparable institutions. The National Preservation Office based in the Library of Congress aims 'to co-ordinate efforts on the part of the Library of Congress to provide direct and indirect service to the library, archive and preservation communities'. It is concerned to 'organize and administer a nationwide library conservation program for all libraries'[26]. Also in the USA, the Northeast Document Conservation Center (formerly the New England Document Conservation Center) offers 'preservation workshops, teaching and training facilities, photoduplication capabilities and field services, plus its staff of experts'[26]. It was the first enterprise of its kind to be created. Much more important, it is entirely a cooperative venture with state subsidies.

Wherever established, any such centre would obviously have to work very closely with the British Library Reference Division Preservation Department. Indeed it is inconceivable that it could be successful without some close association with it. The British Library's position, as expressed at the LISC seminar[12], was that 'were there general support for [Stam's] suggestion the British Library would be ready to respond very positively'[27]. This would doubtless go a long way towards meeting many of the problems involved in establishing such a centre. Ideally it might be established within the British Library, yet structurally independent of it. At all events, the need is real enough and the establishment of a centre seems to demand a high level of priority. Perhaps the next stage is for LISC to consider how this priority might be tackled.

9 Priorities and policies

9.1 Expenditure

Priorities and policies usually go hand in hand. The priorities in any library are certainly a matter of policy, whether as officially expressed by the governing body or as unofficially practised by the librarian and the library staff. The conclusion to be drawn from the questionnaires is either that the priorities attached to conservation are very low or that the finance available does not allow more desirable policies to obtain. In this context it would be useful to learn from those libraries now spending significant sums on conservation (three report spending the equivalent of 90%-100% of their accessions budget on conservation) if this represents an established or recently introduced practice. Expenditure in the British Library, for example, is currently high but this reflects a comparatively new policy. The questionnaires do not reveal this information which will be relevant to a detailed assessment of the national conservation needs.

Given the generally low level of expenditure, the policy which the questionnaire returns point to as prevailing in most libraries is that which has been traditional in British libraries, namely the costs incurred in 'sending books to binding'. This entirely sensible practice was essential to the preservation of periodical parts in volume form, of the earliest forms of paper-back publications and of delapidated stock on the library shelves. It conceals an almost total lack of attention to conservation as it is now understood. It hardly merited a written policy statement and indeed few libraries have one. It did not demand a level of staffing which might be expected in dealing with the complex problems with which we are becoming familiar today. It has for many years been the practice to identify a member of staff responsible for 'binding preparation'. It was never regarded as a demanding responsibility in most libraries to compare with cataloguing, classification and rare book librarianship. This attitude is to some extent responsible for the problems of today. The failure to despatch books for appropriate treatment, or to despatch them at all, the all too frequently low level of staff involved, the lack of adequate direction not only to external but also to in-house binders, these are endemic in the traditional 'binding' approach.

Only in some of the great country houses with book-collector owners have the traditional 'binding' measures proved successful and much of their content predates the invasion of wood-pulp paper. Even so, it is all too often the case that when these libraries find their way into institutions, somehow or other they begin to deteriorate. The University Grants Committee

(UGC) returns cited in the Parry Report[28] identified among university libraries in 1964/5 an average of about 6% of the total library expenditure being devoted to 'binding', the same figure as that produced by the Canadian survey of national libraries during 1982. It is important to recognise here that in many libraries as costs rose and annual accessions grew the amount of binding undertaken remained much the same, so that the percentage of stock treated actually fell. The proportion of stock 'sent to binding' was rarely at any time sufficient to meet more than absolute need. It was never considered as conservation, but as a necessary part of daily library economy. The combined impact of increased use of stock and substantial growth in accessions could never be contained within these measures.

It is instructive to consider the expenditure on 'binding' over the years since the Parry Report as published in the UGC[29] annual returns. They are expressed here firstly as percentages of total expenditure on acquisitions, secondly as percentages of total library expenditure:

	Books and periodicals £	'Binding' £	%	Total expenditure £	%
1965-6	2,493,808	371,744	14.9	6,306,565	5.9
1966-7	3,017,799	442,450	14.7	7,401,028	6.0
1967-8	3,308,600	456,939	13.8	8,161,068	5.6
1968-9	3,801,717	481,734	12.7	9,468,973	5.1
1969-70	4,352,967	528,248	12.1	10,927,118	4.8
1970-1	4,949,815	609,039	12.3	12,683,594	4.8
1971-2	5,846,030	706,389	12.1	14,996,259	4.7
1972-3	6,900,049	804,204	11.7	17,466,222	4.3
1973-4	8,183,777	895,421	11.0	20,582,191	4.4
1974-5	8,955,979	1,034,988	11.6	24,530,880	4.0
1975-6	11,306,913	1,564,299	13.8	31,000,176	5.0
1976-7	13,495,384	1,605,927	11.9	35,880,494	4.5
1977-8	15,307,692	1,794,710	11.7	39,902,383	4.5
1978-9	17,183,700	2,122,800	12.4	46,091,700	4.6
1979-80	18,588,400	2,449,400	13.2	53,787,500	4.6

These figures relate only to expenditure within universities but in the context of the questionnaire returns it is possible to infer general conclusions for all libraries. The inescapable fact is that over 15 years the proportion of expenditure devoted to 'binding' has actually declined and that against a background of inflation 'binding' slipped in the priorities of university libraries. A lower level than that of the affluent 1960s might have been predicted but this was the time when the full weight of the information explosion was reflected in library accessions. It is difficult to believe that the bulk of the 'binding' activity could have been directed to anything other than new stock. 'Conservation' as such must represent a very small proportion of the work done. Even assuming errors of interpretation found in all statistical returns, a very wide measure of tolerance would not change the picture in any significant way.

These assumptions must also apply to the questionnaire returns. The generally low expenditure on conservation becomes that much worse in the light of the 'sending to binding' of current accessions. The libraries spending the equivalent of 90% of their acquisitions budget on conservation are a highly select group. They comprise one national, one college and one public library. The large number spending less than 29% include 162 libraries which spend less than 9%. This conforms entirely to the traditional pattern whereby only essential housekeeping 'binding', not a conservation exercise in itself, is to be found in the expenditure. Even where large in-house binderies exist only a very modest part of their work relates to conservation as such. In the bindery of Cambridge University Library a very small proportion of the total output might be termed conservation, by far the greater proportion being cased, fully sewn, or oversewn bindings of current acquisitions. The same was true of the bindery output in the John Rylands University Library of Manchester[30] during the years 1965-80. It might be concluded that whatever the views of the library staff, certain priorities seem to be unchangeable if the library is to function efficiently. The demands on current literature, especially periodical literature, put a heavy responsibility on the staff to ensure that these demands are met. Whilst preservation of new stock must represent an important element in the conservation picture, it is at most a preventative rather than remedial measure.

Just how ill-equipped libraries are to meet their present conservation needs requires little further comment in the light of the reported expenditure. It is certain that the conservation required, of which libraries generally are now acutely aware, lies outside the scope of the available finance. To make matters worse, it is questionable whether these seemingly essential policies of binding new accessions, printed for the most part on paper which is not acid free, are not viewed in the long term a case of 'throwing good money after bad'. The prospects of libraries introducing or availing themselves of the necessary mass deacidifiction processes to meet the long existing needs on the shelves, let alone new requirements, are remote to say the least. Even the replacement of those highly acidic boxes still to be found on so many library shelves, urgent as such an elementary step must be, costs time and money which has to be found within existing budgets. How many special collection departments have replaced those small slips of paper, acidic markers in otherwise acid-free collections of sermons, tracts, pamphlets, placed there by well-meaning curators in times gone by? Even this most modest of measures has a cost implication.

9.2 Ordering priorities in 'binding'

Priorities relevant to conservation involve considerations and decisions beyond the actual treatment of the stock, important though this is. They raise the basic question, for example, of whether whole categories of stock should be conserved at all. Should conservation priorities be determined by use, the exigencies of daily routines, as already indicated, or should libraries determine to live with alternative methods to the 'binding up' of periodicals and such 'bread and butter' daily fare? Should librarians continue to present readers with 12, 16 or however many articles bound together in one volume when in fact only one is required or are there other less traditional means of securing the stock? Certainly in large libraries, *faute de mieux*, increasing numbers of journals remain unbound. Deposit libraries, despite their primary archival role, have long since been forced to ignore specific categories of accessions for binding purposes. Material coming into the library under the Act[31] is housed in conditions appropriate to good conservation but the finance to meet other conservation measures simply is not available for much of this stock. In the case of the two university copyright libraries this is despite the fact that they consistently head the table for expenditure on 'binding' among universities by a wide margin over the 15 years referred to above. In such closed-access collections ordering priorities even in this most oblique way is a fact of library life. One consequence has been that, for the first-edition-conscious scholarship of today, with its concern for the order of editions, leaving stock in the state published has brought compensations quite lost to the uniformly bound three-decker novels of the 19th century. Other measures have been much more deliberate. When Cambridge University Library decided that all pre-1800 books were of special-collection status and transferred them to closed-access areas of the Library this was a conservation strategy as much as a Library convenience. It removed a whole category of the stock from unsupervised use by any kind of reader and strengthened that other area crucial to preservation, the security of the stock. The loss and mutilation of stock must be very much of concern in any library conservation policy.

Few would question that pre-1800 stock should normally be secured. How many would dissent from the view that all such stock need not necessarily be subject to other conservation treatment? Does every copy of Mrs Inchbold's *Plays*, of Samuel Johnson's *Lives of the English Poets*, of the seventh edition of Richardson's *Pamela* really need to be conserved in the strict sense of the word? Just how many copies of *The Spectator* or *The Guardian* in their various editions exist in numerous libraries may well be revealed by the

ESTC[32]. Should all be subject to expensive conservation treatment? The most important consideration must surely be to see that a number of copies are fully conserved and recorded as such in certain libraries. If cooperation in the production of a list of microform masters and the like is essential, then cooperation between libraries in listing works conserved is no less desirable. In fact, given present limitations of finance, cooperation in this and other ways is likely to become a very important factor in the solution of a very expensive problem. It would seem essential in any database of library holdings, centralised or distributed, that the state of conservation be recorded. It could well be as important to know the state of a book as to discover if a library has a copy of the book at all. Yet, as all librarians know, cooperation of any kind has a price-tag too and even this possible step will have to be weighed in the overall financial balance, find its place in the order of priorities.

9.3 Collection building

It is already seven years since the Atkinson Report[33] clouded the horizons of many a university librarian. It may not have hit its original target but its appearance stimulated much long-overdue thinking and rethinking of library policies. 'Weeding stock' was much referred to and seen as an integral part of one of the mainstays of British librarianship, that is, collection building. Conservation forms an essential element in any collection-building exercise; indeed to omit it would make nonsense of the whole undertaking. It illustrates clearly the all-embracing nature of conservation, touching on so much that is so important in library policy. Decisions on what to buy have their corollary in what to preserve. The two belong very much to one and the same process. Public libraries have long since made local history their undisputed province and, in fact, many returns from these libraries indicated this as a prime field, in some cases the sole field, of preservation activity. Commercial librarianship is equally an area which public libraries have made peculiarly their own but quite different, highly selective views about conservation prevail in this very active area of library use. Most libraries, even the smallest, have their 'special collections' which presumably attract an immediate conservation input. This priority definitely reflects one element of library policy.

The use of staff is a clear way of identifying and expressing priorities. A higher level of priority given to conservation must in any financial situation have implications for existing library staff. Evidence of need can only be marshalled through surveys of stock and the questionnaire shows that these are few and far between. The amount of work to be done, some indication as to costs, must be the starting point for the realisation of any new activity, in libraries or anywhere else. The now retired foreman binder, Mr A May, in the John Rylands University Library of Manchester used to claim that enough work was to be found on the shelves to last him and his staff well into the 21st century, without any further additions to stock. It may have been a counsel of perfection but it was largely on the basis of such a telling statement that overtime money for a Saturday morning refurbishing programme of the rare book stock was made available by the University.

9.4 Local considerations

Need related to potential expenditure is likely to attract attention. This project cannot put any figure on national requirements; suffice it to say that it must run into many millions of pounds. An urgent general priority must be for every library, with the possible exception of the British Library Reference Division, to quantify its individual requirement. There would be little value in announcing to the Library Syndicate in Cambridge University Library that a large injection of funds is necessary to rehabilitate deteriorating stock: facts and figures are of the essence in such a statement. Unfortunately, there are all too many variables in such an assessment. In the absence of mass deacidification possibilities, the cost of deacidifying individual books is very high. A very rough estimate of stock, which has a high acidic content and should be preserved, is beyond many large libraries.

Priorities extend to building construction and atmospheric conditions, and are no less important than priorities of treatment of stock. These are obvious major policy matters, even if no building is in sight. Monitoring stack conditions can be as vital to the welfare of stock as actual conservation treatment. It is a minority activity in terms of the survey. In fact, the evidence on temperature and humidity controls revealed by the questionnaire endorses again the low priority attached to conservation. Air-conditioning, humidity controls, all the atmospheric regulators in new buildings are expensive to install and to operate. Building committees can all too easily override librarians where costs and conditions are concerned and determine an essentially library priority. As with so much in librarianship, a great deal depends on the librarian, his standing in his community, his *persona*, his commitment to the matter in hand and his determination to achieve the right priorities.

9.5 Staff requirements

Priorities presuppose staff capable not only of insisting on them, but, at a more basic level, of identifying and ordering them in day-to-day practice. From both questionnaires it seems that libraries cannot look to new appointments to provide such staff and the past record and state of affairs today is hardly encouraging as far as existing staff are concerned. Priorities relate, therefore, to education of library staff. It will hardly suffice to depend on reorganised priorities within libraries to meet this deficiency. Library educators will have to look to their priorities in terms of their curricula. The training questionnaire identifies unequivocally not so much the low priority but an almost total absence of conservation as a subject within library school courses. Moreover, even if that were otherwise, it indicates that at a technical level there will hardly be the reservoir of trained craftsmen to meet the need in any adequate sense. It suggests that unless present trends within the craft itself are reversed, the future can only be worse than the present. This is in some respect an even more urgent cause for concern than the low priorities existing in the libraries themselves.

Having said that, library schools, colleges of technology and further education respond to the signals they receive and conservation in libraries has hardly been signalled with any sense of urgency until very recent times. As noted elsewhere, library schools are anxious to accommodate the problem; colleges of technology and further education are no less anxious to produce the technical staff required. Whether the same enthusiastic response would be evoked in the knowledge of the maintenance of existing staffing levels, that is as an additional burden on present staff, has not been investigated by the survey. The days of additional staff to meet new developments have in general long since passed. The positions of educators and librarians have a great deal in common in this respect.

The fact is that in libraries, as in most professions, the order of priorities is difficult to change, unless 'new' money is forthcoming. As far as conservation is concerned, almost inevitably viewed by administrators and governing bodies in its traditional 'bindery' mould, the long history of low priority almost insulates against any sudden change in priority. Automation, the application of computers, reflected the widespread use of new technology across society in general and it brought new money. It is difficult to see conservation achieving comparable success. As far as government-funded bodies are concerned, the case will require dramatic presentation to achieve any remote success.

9.6 National heritage

Nevertheless, this should not pre-empt approaches to government and others to raise funds. After all, Lord Brownlow's splendid Restoration home in Lincolnshire, Belton House, has only recently attracted £8 million from the National Heritage Memorial Fund so that the National Trust could acquire it. Nothing could be closer or more crucial to the heritage of the nation than the innumerable manuscripts and printed books housed in libraries across the country. To be realistic the final cost would be much in excess of that figure but it would be a noble start. Accompanied by a judicious review and reordering of priorities within libraries and an examination of cooperative possibilities, the present situation could be drastically altered.

10 International perspective

10.1 The Canadian survey

The objectives of the project were broadened at an early stage to afford an international comparison at least with Western Europe and North America. The intention was to seek information about the main findings of the project from national and selected other libraries and from the principal professional library associations and research organisations. The possibility of achieving this objective by this kind of postal enquiry was put in jeopardy by the size and complexity of the surveys and the time scale of the project. The principal purpose of the project was to assess the situation in the UK and much time was given to discussing and perfecting the main instruments of investigation, the questionnaires.

Fortunately, a number of events took place during the year of the project which, if not removing the desirability of the international comparison, at least took away the urgency of the proposed postal enquiry. First and most important of these was the availability of the report of the survey conducted by the National Library of Canada for the Conference of Directors of National Libraries[34] already cited. It was privately circulated to national libraries in 1982 in typescript form and has not been published through trade channels. It is based on the returns of a questionnaire from 36 of the 65 national libraries circulated, and much of it is highly relevant to this project. The summary of its findings, 'Profile of conservation/preservation activities in the average national library', is incorporated as an annexe to this report. It appears with the kind permission of the Conference, the National Library of Canada and Mrs Missy Hillman who undertook the survey, and whose help and cooperation is warmly acknowledged.

The survey was concerned to identify the position and role of national libraries within their countries. Its questionnaire fell into three parts[34]:

'A. *National perspectives* – intended to describe the conservation/preservation activities in the country;

B. *National library's leadership role* – intended to more closely define the national library's role in conservation/preservation activities among the country's libraries;

C. *Internal conservation/preservation activities* – intended to survey the internal conservation programs of individual national libraries.'

It identified in the international context many of the issues which are very pertinent to this report. Indeed, the present project is probably reflected in the response to one of the questions in Section B. 'Only two national libraries (Poland and Canada) have undertaken formal nationwide surveys. (The Canadian survey, however, was directed to special collections librarians only.) Nationwide surveys have been conducted in three other countries, but these were not done by the national library. Twelve national libraries plan to conduct surveys in the future.'[34] The returns from the national libraries reveal a very marked similarity to the findings of this project (except in the level of return, 55.5%). Even the timing coincides since that survey was commissioned at the 1980 conference which took conservation as its theme. Conservation was by then conclusively an international concern.

The summary speaks plainly for the report and its findings. Apart from references to it elsewhere in this report, only two points need be made here. The first is that the survey shows that 'the average country does not have a national preservation policy for library materials', nor does it have 'an active conservation/preservation program based on that policy'. The second is in respect of the position of the British national library. It emerges clearly that the British Library is generally in advance of the 'average' national library in virtually all the aspects of conservation examined. In regard to staff employed on conservation, for example, it heads the list of employees, followed by France with 160, Turkey 111 and the USA with 107. Again, current expenditure by the British Library on preservation puts it well out of the 'average' league where 'less than 6% of the operating budget is allocated to conservation'. Only in regard to the actual deacidification of stock does it appear to lag behind countries such as the USA and Canada in the acquisition of the appropriate installations and in the mass treatment of stock. However, there may well be very good reason for this. For one thing, unlike the Library of Congress, the British Library has had none of the benefits derived from a space programme. Moreover, mass deacidification is still very much at an experimental stage and the size of the British Library problem demands that the right investment be made. The general conclusion, negative though it may be in some respects, is that the 'state of the art' in the UK is certainly no worse than elsewhere and in most respects much better.

10.2 The Australian scene

Substance was added to the Canadian survey by the opportune appearance of the proceedings of the first of a series of seminars held in the National Library of Australia in February 1982 on 'Managing the library preservation program'. It may well have been prompted by the National

Libraries Conference and again touches on many of the issues raised in the present report. It concludes that 'the development of library preservation programs in Australia is not well advanced; many major Australian libraries have no conservation programs'. In particular it underlines the dearth of hard information about the Australian problem. The following conclusions[35] could well be taken from the present report:

> 'Data is needed on the size, nature and specific requirements of collections.
>
> Mechanisms are necessary for assessing priorities.
>
> Methods are required to facilitate estimating procedures for the allocation of resources.
>
> Attention and effort should be applied to examination and documentation of work patterns.'

The first Australian seminar confirmed in the most direct way the findings of the Canadian survey, supplying a case study of one national library. Significantly, it is the national library which is providing the lead in Australia.

10.3 Awareness

Another event notable for its timing was the appearance early in 1983 of the two volume *Library and archives conservation: 1980 and beyond* by G M and D G Cunha[36], already cited. There may be differing opinions as to the value of this publication but should any evidence be required to demonstrate that this report can only touch specifically on the wider aspects of conservation, that publication certainly will supply it. Volume II is a supplement to the Cunha bibliography contained in their *Conservation of library materials*, 1972[36], and it adds almost 6,000 entries to the 4,882 listed then. Volume I is a descriptive account of the growth of conservation awareness traced through the numerous developments in the 1970s in the USA. It is noted in the introduction to Volume II that 'the information published in the United States in the last few years indicates a greater general awareness on the part of librarians, archivists, curatorial staff, and administrators, and public records managers of the importance of preventive conservation and conservation management for large and small collections of all sorts of records'[36]. It has to be said that the vast amount of preservation activity recorded by Cunha has not found its counterpart 'on the ground' in the UK although a glance at the research centres and professional associations listed for the UK by Cunha as available to librarians and archivists may suggest otherwise. Perhaps it is significant that in the USA librarians, archivists and other interested parties seem to work more closely together than is the case here.

Cunha notes that 'at long last in the 1980s, after a period of almost complete indifference prior to 1960, a spell of increasing awareness of the problem in the 1960s, then a decade of study and investigation in the 1970s, librarians and archivists are taking charge of conservation management in their profession'[36]. The British timetable might be said to be running one decade behind. Since the UK was represented at the UNESCO conference on International Cooperation for the Preservation of the Book held in Florence in 1970 and at the meeting in Copenhagen in 1971 between representatives of the International Federation of Library Associations and the International Council on Archives on the Physical Protection of Books and Documents, it can only be surmised that the urgent nature of the need was not communicated to British librarians. The early 1970s were still days of optimism and expectation, the national library was coming into being, economic constraints had yet to visit libraries. Sadly, they were also days of last opportunities for new developments of the kind so necessary in preservation. Be that as it may, conservation awareness has come to the fore in British librarianship much later than it has in the USA. The Canadian survey suggests that the UK is a more representative country in this respect than is the USA.

There are many reasons which may be adduced as to why British libraries have only recently become concerned about conservation, not least among them being that the situation is still not so serious in the UK as in the USA. Among other reasons, possibly one of the most important is that for all their similarities there are nevertheless substantial differences between British and American libraries. Collection development, which must be crucial to preservation policies, has only in the comparatively recent times of financial pressure become selective in the British sense in the USA. It is and has been a way of life in the UK even among the copyright deposit libraries. Big has not been synonymous with good and the immediate consequence is that bad though the situation in the UK may appear to be, book selection has saved libraries from a much worse situation. The different environment in the UK from that of the USA, the extent and variety of library provision, their historical development and other kinds of educational targets all point to a problem of a different order. Much new library building in Britain, especially in universities, has been greatly influenced by the American design. It is significant that more problems of conservation are encountered today in the new, well-lit, warm, air-conditioned buildings than were ever met with in their 'old-fashioned' predecessors. Libraries have survived well in British country houses because they were underheated, subject to normal atmospheric conditons in ill-lit rooms and, of course, in general under-used.

10.4 An American perspective

A further event supplying an international dimension to the project was the visit, early in 1983, of Dr D Stam of New York Public Library. He was invited by the British Library R&D Department to carry out a three-week-long investigation 'from the perspective of American experience' of the conservation situation in the British Library and to some extent in libraries generally. It resulted in his report *National preservation planning in the United Kingdom: an American perspective*[37]. This identifies many areas of activity where American practices might be applicable in the UK and in some respects provides a useful means of comparison between the present state of conservation in both countries. Yet while there is no doubt that some of the American experience should prove valuable in the UK, it is essential that this should be considered against the background of a thorough appraisal of the implications for conservation of the basic differences in policies and styles of British and American librarianship. Not least it has to be seen against the background of the finance available, the methods of funding the libraries and the urgent need in the UK for basic provision before contemplating some of the more advanced possibilities opened up by Dr Stam.

The answer to most library problems lies in funding, in conservation no less than any other area of library activity. This has a truly international dimension. In all libraries, conservation is one potential source of expenditure, competing within the overall budget with a whole variety of other claims. None of the technical conservation processes or substitutes for the book is cheap nor is likely to become so, unlike computer hardware. Indeed, in conservation, cheapness is almost a prescription for trouble and it can be said with certainty that many of the future problems of conservation will derive directly from the cheaper processes involved in modern book production. The main lesson from the international scene is that not only can individual libraries not 'go it alone' but librarianship will need to look outside itself to its sister profession, archives, and to others in the general field of conservation. Cooperation has been a much over-used and devalued word in librarianship but it is difficult to see how any solution to the immense problems of conservation can be achieved without it. Here the American example has much to commend it. Coordination of conservation effort might go a long way towards achieving a national plan.

11 Conclusions

11.1 The preservation position

The findings of the two questionnaires, the discussion within the Project Committee, the interviews by the Research Assistant and Project Director with archivists, librarians and other interested parties, the proceedings of the LISC and Cambridge seminars and the very wide exposure achieved by the project allow a number of specific conclusions to be drawn about preservation in British libraries. It is quite clear that most of what has been suspected hitherto about conservation in libraries, both practices and policies, can be statistically verified. It is equally clear that the concern among librarians is real and that there is a general desire that 'something must be done'. Perhaps most important of all, there is evidently an atmosphere in which not only something can be done but all the interested parties seem prepared to participate in bringing it about. This is true even though the chances of any substantial changes or improvements in funding may be slight.

Some of the main conclusions can be listed as follows:

(1) There is today widespread and growing interest in and concern for preservation in all types of library.

(2) There is recognition at the highest levels in library administration of the urgent need for preservation policies.

(3) There is an almost total absence of formal written conservation policies in libraries and widespread uncertainty about conservation policies in general except negatively among those few libraries proposing to retain none of their stock permanently.

(4) There is no pattern in the ordering of priorities of preservation measures either in individual libraries or nationally; priorities operate on an *ad hoc* basis; priority options are not considered.

(5) There is no sign of national planning for conservation, nor of cooperation or a coordinated approach.

(6) There are in general low levels of expenditure (as a proportion of overall spending) and therefore a low order of priority even among those libraries with conservation/binding elements in their budgets (with the notable exception of the British Library and a very few others).

(7) There is a minority of libraries, only, capable of adjusting fully environmental controls; many libraries do not monitor stack

conditions: two-thirds have no systematic procedure for shelf surveys of stock; not all environmental hazards are recognised in all libraries.

(8) There are in-house binderies and conservation workshops in a minority of libraries; the majority rely on external facilities for all types of work; most libraries use library staff to oversee binding/conservation arrangements but not normally as a senior staff responsibility.

(9) There is a general awareness of the potential of microform as a conservation measure but costs usually restrict use to specific items as need arises; there are virtually no 'microform preservation' programmes in libraries; only a few libraries have appropriate microform production and storage facilities.

(10) There is general approval for a self-financing national centre to advise libraries and to promote research but uncertainty as to its funding, status and location; almost half the libraries already make use of existing scientific expertise; the majority do not subscribe to conservation journals.

(11) There is no evidence of a coordinated approach to scientific or technical research either between libraries themselves or between libraries and those carrying on relevant research outside librarianship.

(12) There is little evidence of conservation training among newly recruited professionally qualified library staff at any level, and there is little provision for conservation in the curricula of library schools or in the minority of higher and further education colleges which cater for library staff.

(13) There is no less inadequate provision for the training of binders and conservators; comparatively few colleges of higher and further education include binding/conservation at an appropriate level; the changed conditions of apprenticeships have not improved preservation prospects in libraries.

(14) There is little understanding among many library staff and less among readers about their conservation role; few libraries provide in-house training for staff; some give basic instruction to users in the handling of books.

(15) There are very few libraries which have any kind of contingency plans formulated to meet emergencies, large or small.

11.2 Unpreparedness

There are further conclusions to be drawn from the investigation but these are of immediate and most pressing concern. Perhaps the most alarming is the simple state of unpreparedness evident in most libraries and the uncertainty among librarians as to what to do or even where to start. Very few libraries have made any real assessment of their problems, either in regard to their size or to the order of priorities nor have they, by and large, contemplated how such an assessment is to be achieved: there is no precedent for it in library administration. Only security, the introduction of precautions to safeguard the stock, has received any widespread attention and this has rarely been considered as a conservation measure. The Atkinson Report[38] produced an angry response from teachers, researchers and librarians in universities when the steady-state library and relegation of stock was proposed. It was claimed that weeding stock was widely practised and that the remaining stock was essential to institutional scholarship. If that is so, it is all the more urgent that steps be taken to preserve it, otherwise there will be a solution not foreseen by the Atkinson Committee. There is little virtue in retaining stock if it is in no fit condition to be used.

The problems implicit in these conclusions cannot all be solved together. Some are likely to be resistant to the only real solution, the injection of significant additional funds, for the foreseeable future. The time to do something, however, is opportune since society at large has never been more preservation conscious. The Clean Air Act, issues of lead-free petrol, protection of the environment, pollution politics, all make for a receptive hearing for any kind of preservation activity. When the particular activity can be related to the national heritage, in this case the national archive of printed books and manuscripts, that becomes so much more relevant and likely to attract attention. The amount of propaganda already put out on preservation has done much to prepare the way for conservation action in libraries. Nor should it be overlooked that archivists, certainly in the public sector, have done much to establish conservation as an important element in planned expenditure.

11.3 Policy matters

In all respects it is something of a 'last chance' policy now confronting libraries. The arrival of the 'brittle book' problems, now so acute in the USA, has been delayed or rather not accelerated by different environmental conditions. It will not pass British libraries by and as Dr Stam indicates it is simply a matter of time. It may even emerge as an immediate threat once conservation surveys have been commenced and some real idea of the state of preservation established. On the positive side it is important to note among these general conclusions the immense influence which established collection development policies in the shape of book selection have had on the preservation problem. Such an established procedure is one of various traditional library practices which along with good housekeeping play a major part in all preservation policies.

12 Recommendations

12.1 Recognition of the problem

The way forward will be determined by the importance which librarians themselves attach to preservation and by the priorities which they accord it. It is clear from the response to the project that the will to secure recognition for conservation is already in being. The LISC Seminar on Conservation in June 1983 and the Dissemination Seminar[12] for the project held in September 1983 were both well attended, produced much positive thinking and contributed significantly to stimulating conservation awareness. The press and the media generally have found the subject not without interest. These may well be instrumental in bringing the conservation needs into those quarters where in the last resort additional library expenditure has to be sought.

12.2 Executive action: local strategy

The findings point to many possible recommendations, some more urgent than others. These will be briefly discussed and then summarised. They fall into clear categories. First of all, there are those steps which librarians can achieve within their own library without reference to additional funding. These could take immediate effect and could constitute a start to a written conservation policy. A prime prerequisite here, which has to be emphasised, is that the librarian himself is fully aware of the need, is seized of the problem and, above all, is determined to come to grips with it. A preservation programme will necessitate, on the evidence of the questionnaires, the introduction of a virtually new dimension into library administration. No such innovation is possible without the absolute commitment of the librarian. It is essential to establish conservation as a way of library life, as an important aspect of the daily routines of the library at all staffing levels. There is little to be gained by concentrating on library assistants reshelving stock, for example, when cleaners are handling books in great quantities, oblivious to the conservation need, or if senior staff are not convinced of its importance.

The librarian, as a pre-condition, has to achieve as much preservation awareness within the library as possible. This may take the form of amending basic routines so that stock is scrutinised on being returned to the shelves, during shelf tidying, as part of the annual inspection; of providing in-house training in conservation for new recruits and existing staff at all levels; of giving regular emphasis to the importance of preservation measures in staff meetings, staff bulletins and library reports; of producing printed guide-lines on book-handling; of purchasing conservation manuals and taking out subscriptions to appropriate journals; of publishing a general guide to readers on book-handling, within and outside the library; and of mounting exhibitions of damaged, ill-used books. There are many such possibilities. Conservation is all-embracing in its implications, a matter for all the staff of the library not simply the conservators and binders or that member of the library staff 'responsible' for it. That is not to say that these staff have nothing to learn. On the contrary, it is particularly important that they grasp the library side of the problem, that they see the whole conservation picture. Much avoidable damage has been caused by binders acting in good but misguided faith in the past. It has to be accepted that even the best conservation measures can be undermined by the failure of staff to recognise the problem. Photocopying in the wrong hands can damage the best conservation work: not only authors and publishers have cause for concern over self-service photocopying machines. In the words of one respondent: 'Photocopying is the worst enemy of books'.

None of the measures cited here, and it is by no means an exhaustive list, depends upon additional funding but is within the immediate executive action of the librarian. Also within the immediate responsibility of the librarian is the preparation of agendas and papers for meetings of the library's governing body. His or her influence in policy matters is usually decisive and the responsibility of bringing conservation before governors and other policy-makers, an essential step if the appropriate policy for conservation is to be secured, rests with the librarian. In view of the widespread relevance of conservation in a library's affairs, impinging on so many aspects of the administration, there are many opportunities for raising it. Collection building, though essentially the librarian's immediate responsibility, is in the end a policy matter. The strength of collections, subject development, decisions on relegation or disposal, are of interest to more than librarians as the reception of the Atkinson Report demonstrated. A decision to retain everything is very much a policy matter and, like acquisition, fundamental to a preservation policy. Though such a decision may have become policy long ago, the present cost implications of such a preservation policy are new and should find their way on to agendas as a matter of urgency. Similarly, preservation microfilming is an expensive undertaking if carried out systematically and, however desirable, will compete with established library expenditure. Ideally, additional monies should be sought but if the only way to obtain them is by re-ordering priorities, this is still a policy matter. All are matters which, finally, if only in the form of a report, should appear on the agendas of governing bodies. All such issues, if aired in committee, will help to generate conservation awareness and condition those concerned with finance to the need for and cost of conservation. It is very much to be hoped for these very reasons that this project also will find its way on to the agendas of such bodies.

Another purely in-house initiative lies in the production of a contingency plan to meet disasters, large or small. This is, quite literally, a statement of the procedures to be followed by the library staff in the event of an emergency. It involves much planning aimed both at emergency prevention and at emergency procedures. It tones up normal maintenance programmes since many minor disasters may well find their origins there. In short, it does for the library stock what health and safety measures are doing for library staff. Certainly, however remote it may seem, disasters in libraries cannot be ignored, as librarians who have experienced them recognise only too well. To fire and flood are to be added the threats of vandalism and terrorism of modern society. It affects the planning of new buildings and the replanning of old. It is with the greatest difficulty, for example, that architects and planners are dissuaded from installing sprinkler systems, the concomitant installation of smoke detectors in new library buildings. Disaster planning calls not only for an assessment of the resources within the library but for facilities in the immediate area which might be called on should they be needed, such as deep-freeze or cold-storage facilities, freeze drying vacuum chambers and fumigation possibilities. In Cambridge, where a network of important libraries exists outside the University Library, there is much scope for cooperation based on the University Library's 'disaster plan'. In fact, it is currently being extended outside the libraries of the university and colleges into the region. It has all the making of a successful piece of library cooperation and, having had unfortunately already two opportunities to test the system, can be said to work. This is not the place for detailed discussion of a subject which is becoming well documented in the literature. It must, however, be recognised as an important aspect of preservation and certainly a matter involving policy decisions in governing bodies.

Much of this so far might be termed local strategy. It is an essential prerequisite, however, to any formulation of policy within the library. If any policy decisions on conservation are to be made, they can only take place in an atmosphere of conservation awareness. That means more than the awareness of senior librarians, heads of conservation and specific staff involved. From all that has been said it follows that the policy must be to introduce and accept preservation as a normal charge on the library's budget of comparable importance to other major library activities. It must also go beyond administrative routines and conservation technology to encompass environmental controls where necessary and possible. There will clearly be different requirements in libraries aiming to retain different quantities of stock permanently but the initial treatment of stock coming into all libraries must have a common preservation requirement. Even libraries aiming to dispose of all stock eventually will be unable to escape the collapse of much-used stock in perfect bindings before its useful life in the library is over. The strengthening of such publications, whether by cut-flush bindings or some such method of 'Lyfguarding', is conservation and in such libraries, no less than in those aiming to retain a proportion of stock permanently, has its place among priorities. The most important element of policy, however, for those institutions proposing to retain no stock permanently, is to ensure that it is disposed of, where still sound, to an appropriate recipient.

12.3 Priorities within the library

Policies involve priorities both within the priorities of the library in general and within the priorities of conservation itself. With regard to the former it is difficult to separate them from finance, in fact priorities in libraries are generally reflected by order of expenditure. Conservation is an expensive business. Lack of adequate funds and staff to meet even essential conservation is a constant theme in the questionnaire responses which was also repeated loudly at the two seminars. An immediate first step must be to establish a comparison of the costs of conservation with those of cataloguing, classification, inter-library loans, automated activity and other recognised kinds of expenditure. Conservation is unlikely to displace acquisition from its prime position in the budget nor, since it is in one sense the absolute prerequisite for all conservation, should it aim to do so, but here too comparison of expenditure is valuable. Since virement between heads of expenditure may not be possible, conservation has to be shown for what it is, a new development in terms of the budget to be placed on a funding par with many other library activities. It is recognised that the times are not propitious to seek 'new' monies but it is hoped that this report may arrive on the desks of treasurers, administrators, members of management committees and governing bodies as well as on those of librarians. This report and the current example of the British Library in meeting its conservation needs could represent a major plank in the argument of any library seeking such funding.

Priorities within conservation itself are easier to achieve and in part at least are self-determining. It is in the nature of their different roles that priorities will differ from one institution to another. However, all libraries can despatch books to conservation which are returned to issue desks and are both in need of attention and worth preserving. This has the advantage of bringing conservation attention to the 'active' stock, which in some respects is most at risk. As noted earlier, libraries which practise 'annual inspection' or regular 'shelf tidying', can also include conservation surveillance within this activity. In rare-book and manuscript collections, piecemeal inspection of stock shelf by shelf throughout the year can be introduced on a daily or weekly basis. This has the great merit of introducing security checks as well as ensuring preservation of the more valuable stock. Ideally, a conservation survey should be put in hand but the same aims can be achieved gradually in the way described over a period. The whole picture does not emerge at once and to some extent this must be a disadvantage, but at least the conservators and binders will not object to that. There is also the question of treatment. It has to be acknowledged that few if any libraries with large special collections can afford to treat all the items in need of attention. This being so, there is a great deal to be said in the treatment of rare books and manuscripts for the use of the individually constructed acid-free case or box. It is cheaper, quicker, eliminates problems of obliterating provenance and is frequently easier for the reader to use. It can also look good. This is particularly true of the traditional box with the folding spine, often appropriately covered to match the content. It does not represent necessarily a postponed binding; on the contrary, it has distinct bibliographical advantages from the scholarly point of view. The late K Povey, librarian of Liverpool University, designed cheap, fold-away boxes for holding issues of periodical literature. It met with little enthusiasm at the time from the generation of librarians who had bound miles of periodicals 'to pattern'. It is worth further exploration today, both on grounds of preservation and of cost. Periodical binding consumes a large proportion of slender conservation budgets. More flexible and adaptable to the individual volume is the temporary box designed by the Library of Congress, the so-called 'phase box'. It is becoming widely used. Boxing materials has always found a place, perhaps reluctantly, in preservation programmes and at the very least it avoids irreparable damage due to good but mistaken intentions. If considered not as a temporary substitute for binding, but as a permanent alternative, it could well provide the financial leeway in budgets to conserve books with higher priority.

Two other measures of self-help may be considered. It has been seen that many libraries rely on external trade binderies to meet many of their needs, and that such binders hold a key position in any national preservation programme. A code of practice for both binders and libraries, on the despatch, handling and treatment of books, is highly desirable if not essential for all concerned. Not all staff responsible for 'preparation for binding' in libraries will be equipped with all the necessary conservation knowledge. Not all binders receiving work will always recognise when special treatment is required. Most necessary for these transactions are rules or basic instructions on limits of action and types of materials. Frequently, all too little contact exists between customer and client. Second is the production of a conservation statement on the library's priorities and policies. Although originating with the librarian, this is certainly a matter for wide staff participation, both from the professional library and conservation technical sides. Few library activities touch the interests of so many library departments as conservation does. The compilation itself can make a major contribution to conservation awareness with the library. It is crucial to collection development.

12.4 National cooperative possibilities

Opportunities for action outside libraries are no less real than those within. The need for cooperation measures, at national and local levels, has been touched on frequently in this report. There is no national plan for preservation and this raises various policy questions. Foremost among these are the proposals indicated by libraries for retention of stock. As noted earlier, the size of the preservation problem must inevitably relate to the quantity of books it is intended to preserve. The number of libraries proposing to retain considerable amounts of stock permanently poses directly the problem of national priorities and can only be resolved in that connection. The answer of the universities to the Atkinson Committee on retention of stock was that holdings reflected and were determined by the patterns of teaching and research in their institutions. The 73 public libraries aiming to retain over 80% of their stock will have no such justification. Whatever the local reasons it seems difficult to accept such ambitious intentions unquestioningly as part of a national preservation plan.

The concern to establish priorities within a national plan was emphasised at the 1983 Cambridge Dissemination Seminar. Well-known special collections urgently in need of attention might be neglected if priority listings were not provided. It seemed an essential first step to identify important collections so that they might receive special attention. Again, it was noted that whilst the total stock of public libraries was of questionable value as a subject of preservation, their special collections, usually comprising important local history items or materials unique to the locality, would be especially apposite. The further identification and assessment of such special needs was one possible approach to the ordering of priorities within a national policy. The proposals on stock retention revealed by the questionnaire could hardly form the basis of a national policy.

There are other aspects to national policies apart from stock retention, important as this must be. Education and training in preservation as in most other activities are at the heart of the problem. It was clear from both librarians and educators that conservation for librarians barely features in the present curricula of library schools. No-one should be in doubt that the maintenance, treatment and handling of stock is as vital in library service as the cataloguing and classifying of it. Anxiety was expressed at the Cambridge Seminar at 'the switch from books to computers' in the education of librarians, that the place of the book in library school curricula was threatened even more by the growth in information technology. Whether through management, historical bibliography or rare book courses, the book should be restored to its rightful place in the education of librarians and conservation was another means of achieving that. There is evidence in the returns that the schools of librarianship do not have to be convinced of this or the need for conservation training and are anxious to introduce instruction whether at undergraduate or postgraduate level. It is important to repeat that librarians with conservation knowledge not specialist conservators are required. This provision could probably be achieved within existing resources or at worst with only a modest increase in library school costs.

Much the same is true of the training of binders and conservators, the staff at the bench. There is every reason to believe that considerable expansion and rationalisation of existing provision is urgently necessary. Thirty-two institutions concerned with educating librarians and training craftsmen for the whole of the UK is hardly excessive. Indeed, in view of the information disclosed about the contents of courses, it can only be described as minimal. There should be opportunities here for libraries to play a positive part in promoting one of the oldest of the crafts which already has such a distinguished history on library shelves. This brings, however, other factors into consideration in addition to training opportunities, in particular the levels of remuneration which will attract recruits into binding and conservation work. There is little relation between the journeyman's wages working in a library and the value of his contribution to the long-term welfare of the place. Recognition of the importance of conservation also recognises the value to be placed on those conserving the stock. It seems wrong-headed, not to say perverse, that young, newly qualified graduate staff should have salary prospects exceeding those of an experienced manager of an in-house bindery and conservation workshop on whom so much of the future welfare of the institution will depend. It seems almost absurd when in years to come some of his products are likely to take their place among the fine bindings in the special collections of the library.

There must be no doubt as to the crucial importance of this issue in achieving conservation success. In the present difficult times of unemployment, recruiting graduate staff is difficult only because of the numerous applications: recruiting good craftsmen or a foreman binder remains as difficult as ever it has been in the post-war period. In this same context it is important to close the gap between the historians of binding and the current practitioners. Since many of those now highly prized 'contemporary' bindings were in effect the trade products of their day, some closer attention by scholarly bibliographers to today's craftsmen and their work might be expected. Equally important is that the emergent profession of highly qualified conservation consultants should identify with the traditional craft. Similarly, those specialised craftsmen producing consciously artistic modern bindings seem to stand apart from the trade in general. These 'specialists' are representative of the highest traditions and expertise of the craft, not separate from it, and are in a peculiarly influential position, through their links of patronage, to lend great strength to its promotion. It was observed at the Cambridge Seminar that binding was what libraries had, conservation was what they needed, that the two are not the same, and there is some truth in that. Yet whilst it may be true that all binders are not necessarily conservators, it would be difficult to argue that conservators are not also binders. The conservator brings new scientific information and standards to an old craft and is in a position to avoid that sort of damage which binders have unwittingly inflicted on the books they sought to preserve. The fact is that binders need conservators and that the latter cannot hope to meet today's difficulties without marshalling and directing the efforts of the former. It is for that reason that in libraries where conservation has developed, it has usually been grafted on to the bindery in the shape of a new head. Paradoxically, whilst binding doubtless with all its faults can survive without the new science of conservation, the latter needs binding expertise if it is to meet the needs of libraries in any positive sense.

12.5 The trade and industry

The crucial position of the book trade in the present conservation crisis does not bear close examination. After all, it was industry and the trade not the library customer which introduced wood-pulp paper, with all its implications for the acid content of books, and which popularised 'paper backs' and perfect bindings. It has to be accepted that libraries might have acquiesced but theirs was no innovative role, a sin of omission rather than of commission. From the invention of printing, the quality in book production has been on the downward slope, with some honourable distinguished exceptions. Whilst it can be claimed that the 20th century has put books into the range of everyone's pocket, albeit only for a time, it has also put enormous and still increasing burdens on those institutions preserving the national archive of printed materials or providing any research material in depth. Yet only rarely are there meetings between the trade and the customer unless some controversial issues, usually involving legislation, such as the Public Lending Act or a new Law of Copyright, are being discussed. When Gladstone detailed the costs involved in purchasing and preserving books, he complained about the cost of binding, about 'prices fabulously high'[39] for cheap publications; he could not have envisaged the problems faced by libraries today.

It is all rather reminiscent of Updike's[40] conclusions on book production: 'All along, the changes in books were influenced by commercial conditions. The first books were folios – large and dear. What did the printer do? He produced books which were small and cheap, and we have the Aldine 16mo volumes, printed in italic (a letter adopted chiefly because it was compact), for their period perfectly commercial though attractive editions. Again,

Pigouchet and Vérard at Paris printed their Books of Hours, and they were very charming volumes. They were not as charming as the manuscripts from which they were copied, but they were far, far cheaper. By and by, when printers discovered the ignorance of the public and its willingness to buy books however badly printed, they dared to make them poorer and poorer. They printed what we call "good" books, because ours are worse; but what they thought were poor ones, because older books had been so much better. This they did because they could sell them, and because they did not even then realize what we know now – how wretchedly books can be made and still be sold!'.

The book trade is not responsible for the paper and printing industries any more than libraries are for booksellers and publishers. It is, however, in a position to decide on the products and methods of book production which it wishes to employ. The book trade has to be educated to look beyond the short-term advantages of perfect binding and to recognise how great a contribution it could make to conservation in the papers it uses and the bindings it produces. The need for acid-free paper has not gone entirely unnoticed by the trade: more and more the legend 'printed on permanent/durable paper with a neutral pH', or something similar is to be found behind the title page of new books. The possibility of deposit copies for copyright libraries on acid-free paper, even of legislation to attain such an objective, has often been mooted. It would constitute a modest improvement in the context of the national archive of printed materials but the preservation requirements go far beyond that. The cost implications of such runs, also, would probably be greater than if all the copies were printed on acid-free paper.

Progress on these issues in the USA will be watched with interest. The Bailey Committee on Production Guidelines for Book Longevity published an interim report in 1981[41]. It suggests that publishers may well find sound economic reasons to publish on acid-free paper. Some support for this view; is to be found among British publishers. It emerged at the Cambridge Seminar from the background to another British Library investigation[42] that publishers were often unaware of different types of paper and had no knowledge of the effects on book life of acid-free paper. Frequently they used it without knowing that it was acid free. Paper makers too were moving towards an alkaline system which made available a competitively priced 'permanent' paper. A representative of the Production Committee of the Publishers Association, which is also looking into the use of acid-free paper, saw no reason not to use it if increased costs were not involved.

It would be misleading not to acknowledge that much research in paper science, leather technology and related book materials is being carried out both by industry and in institutions of higher education. As a result we know about acid hydrolysis in paper, oxidative degradation of the cellulose in paper, the properties of adhesives and much else besides. Part of the conservation problem is to focus all this knowledge and research into a practical programme of preservation easily digestible by librarians. The display of scholarly scientific conservation knowledge at the Cambridge 1980 Conference to the vast majority of practising librarians perusing the proceedings is like giving the earliest aviators a glimpse of the American Shuttle programme. The American library world is forging contacts between all the interested parties. In the UK the British Library has been almost alone in seeking to bridge this gap. Now LISC has shown initiative and its interest in the conservation field by its 1983 seminar. Perhaps LISC or the Office of Arts and Libraries itself is best placed to coordinate the interests of scientific research and the book trade for the benefit of conservation.

12.6 New media

The use of substitutes for the book as a preservation measure – microform, optical disc storage, the many possibilities of the new technology – requires little further comment here. Its importance has been emphasised earlier and it is much discussed in the literature. Much of its potential cannot yet be fully measured or its usefulness interpreted, not least because the technology is in a period of almost constant change. It is obviously important that all progress should be monitored, but at this stage only microform can be safely said to offer a realistic alternative. In this context there is much to commend one American initiative. The *National register of microform masters*[43] is an exercise in cooperative activity which could well be complemented by a similar register in the UK. Dr Stam's view is that a British contribution to the American scheme would be important and welcome. Provided that British libraries did not participate directly in the American register at the expense of the British and that a finding list, not an AACR2 catalogue-style entry, was the object, the proposal should be pursued. Just how many of the existing masters have been filmed to the necessary archival standard and would be usable is another matter altogether. The main contributor to such a register would be the British Library Reference Division in the first instance. The Lending Division's collection of master films of British university theses is also obviously relevant and may well be complemented by master copies of out-of-copyright materials.

The creation of such a National Register illustrates well one of the roles which a National Advisory and Research Centre might undertake. It could also provide basic preservation enquiry services, on the role of the new media for example, and promote for preservation purposes the activities of other specialist bodies such as the National Reprographic Centre for documentation. It would be valuable in a variety of ways. The suitability, availability and costs of microfilm-reading machines were matters of considerable importance in the discussions held by the British Library Working Party on Access to Newspapers. There are among those matters of abiding interest to all librarians and no more so than in the context of preservation. The fact that on this occasion the Working Party's newsletter acted as a channel of communication for an important agent in preservation is itself instructive and underlines the need for a national centre. It may be noted again that the systematic microfilming of materials is likely to prove prohibitively expensive, unless commercial exploitation makes it worthwhile, as for example in the wholesale microfilming of the manuscripts of Trinity College, Cambridge.

12.7 Environmental conditions

Microforms are heavily dependent on environmental controls. The questionnaire revealed much disquieting information about environmental conditions generally in libraries and about the appreciation of the problem by some librarians. An important requirement is to provide guide-lines, preferably in broad-sheet form, for reference purposes in libraries. Some libraries evidently exist in conditions which can only hasten the process of deterioration. Preventative measures are the key to successful preservation and in many libraries are likely to be the only means available for some considerable time. An authoritative statement on minimum requirements, issued for example by LISC, may well persuade governing bodies to look afresh at their own libraries and, if necessary, find the necessary finance to improve conditions. The University Grants Committee seeks to ensure through an appropriate sub-committee that environmental controls are included in all new library buildings. Unfortunately, not all libraries will have new buildings nor access to such a body and it is essential that existing buildings have the right environment for preservation of stock. It is also important that 'fail-safe' measures be devised to meet plant failures in new buildings. Published guide-lines could lead to significant improvements of existing provision.

12.8 National Advisory and Research Centre

Such issues must be linked with proposals for a National Advisory and Research Centre. It emerges plainly from the research that there is no coordinating agency among the numerous and various activities relating to conservation. It was clear from the response that a centre to meet such a need, with the possible funding described earlier in this report, is thought to be highly desirable. The role of the British Library has to be considered here: in any national preservation programme it is bound to be a dominant one. Its leadership has brought preservation both as an element of library policy and 'on the ground' to its present level of recognition nationally. The magnitude of its preservation needs (estimated at £24-30 million of arrears for the Reference Division alone) must point to a concentration of experience and expertise unique in the UK. The Library is also unique in having the resources to tackle the many and varied problems. The major investigations into specific aspects of conservation currently funded by the Reference Division, which are of direct relevance to the needs of all libraries, identify the Library's contribution in factual terms. The many investigations mounted also by the Research and Development Department, of which the present project is one, confirm the Library's leading role, if confirmation were necessary.

The proposal to establish a centre, a focal point for conservation effort and need, reflects the sense of anxiety felt generally over the present situation. It is difficult to envisage a centre divorced from the conservation contribution of the British Library. Many divergent views have been expressed. Whether as some think it should be apart from the British Library, or, as others believe, within it, or yet again within it but structurally independent of it, or any of the other options expressed, is not for this report to determine. Perhaps a detailed examination of the feasibility of such a centre falls within the remit of LISC or the Office of Arts and Libraries. At all events it should be given a high priority.

12.9 The solution

Throughout the project the need for additional funding to meet what is essentially a new library need has been emphasised repeatedly from all sides. It would not be possible to ignore this overwhelming requirement and produce a report which does not recommend the provision of additional funding as a matter of urgency. The fact is that there is a crisis, the national heritage is at risk and it cannot be secured on the basis of existing resources. Yet that is not the whole answer. The conservation problem is a national one and it will not be solved by any one library or by a simple injection of funds, useful though these would be. It will depend on cooperation, on the goodwill of libraries working together and on the contribution of the educators in library schools and colleges. Librarians, their professional organisations and specialist groups should look for closer ties with archivists, the sister profession. They should explore the valuable work now being carried out by the Museums and Galleries Commission in its very different but still highly relevant fields of conservation. The work of the

Area Museums Councils[44] alone is such as to command attention from librarians, suggesting both a model or pattern for future library action and the possibilities of cooperative action. There must be much closer relations with the Publishers Association, the Society of Authors, the book trade, industry and the research organisations. Cooperation exists outside the field of librarianship. The new technology was revolutionary in one sense in the way computers and automation became part of a very traditional profession, establishing links with bodies outside librarianship. It should not be difficult to work more closely with those industrial, trade and professional concerns which are so closely involved in the production of the materials libraries need to conserve.

12.10 Summary of recommendations

12.10.1 Activities within individual libraries

Libraries should:

1) seek to inculcate conservation as a major policy matter in their governing body and among other policy makers (conservation impinges on virtually all aspects of library activity and, given an appropriate order of priority, is very much a policy matter);

(2) aim to create conservation awareness in all library staff at all levels as part of daily routines (in-house instruction in conservation is one of the various means of achieving this described in the report);

(3) express conservation requirements in budgetary terms within library priorities, either seeking new monies or proposing changes in existing patterns of expenditure;

(4) introduce conservation surveys of stock as part of normal routines within the pattern of management;

(5) formulate plans, if possible, in cooperation with other local libraries on a regional basis to meet emergency situations affecting stock, both preventative and remedial measures;

(6) review binding, rebinding and repair procedures, with particular reference to the use of acid-free boxes, and establish effective procedures for the commissioning of work with binders, in-house or external, to preclude the possibilities of damaging stock;

(7) compile a conservation statement on the library's policy.

12.10.2 *Cooperative activities*

Libraries should:

(1) press for the inclusion of education in conservation within the curricula of library schools through the appropriate professional associations;

(2) promote training for binders and conservators in appropriate educational institutions and seek adequate career structures with progressive salary scales for binders and conservators commensurate with their status and importance;

(3) seek to bring preservation requirements before the book-trade, paper, printing and allied industries, alerting the relevant trade and professional bodies such as the Publishers' Association, PIRA, the Institute of Paper Conservation, BPIF[45], and noting the modest success achieved in the USA in this connection;

(4) establish guide-lines for librarians on minimum standards in dealing with binders and produce a basic manual for library staff on conservation, including types of bindings and their suitability;

(5) create a National Register of Microform Masters and in so doing aim to improve standards of production, introduce bibliographic controls and encourage cooperative action;

(6) promote coordination of conservation effort not only between libraries but also with the archives profession and others with related conservation interests;

(7) examine possibilities of cooperation in existing areas of activity such as collection development (with reference to American models) and in new areas such as instruction courses for existing library staff, at local and national level;

(8) emphasise the standards of environmental controls necessary to conservation and indicate 'fail-safe' measures where controls exist, not forgetting the needs of 'new media';

(9) urge that a means of mass-deacidification available on a cooperative basis, and other equipment, essential to conservation, such as appropriate photographic facilities, be provided;

(10) press for the establishment of a national advisory and research centre.

13 References

1. Amman, J. *Panoplia omnium illiberalium mechanicarum aut sedentariarum artium genera continens*, etc, Francofurti ad Moenum, Sigismundi Feyrabendij, 1568.
2. *Figaro*, No 164, 1982, pp 178-9.
3. International Conference on the Conservation of Library and Archive Materials and the Graphic Arts, *Abstracts & preprints*, Cambridge, Society of Archivists & Institute of Paper Conservation, 1980. See also Appendix 3, Papers produced by Steering Committee members, Ratcliffe, *The scientific aspects of conservation*.
4. Banks, P N. Preservation of library materials in *Encyclopaedia of library and information science*, Vol 23, New York, Marcel Dekker, Inc, 1978, pp 180-222; *A selective bibliography on the conservation of research library materials*, Chicago, Newberry Library, 1981.
5. Cunha, G M and D G. *Conservation of library materials*, Metuchen, N J, Scarecrow Press, 1972, 2 vols; *Library and archives conservation: 1980s and beyond*, Metuchen, N J, Scarecrow Press, 1983.
6. Metcalf, K D. *Planning academic and research library buildings*, New York, McGraw Hill, 1965, p 131.
7. University Grants Committee. *Report of the Committee on Libraries*, London, HMSO, 1967, p 92.
8. The flooding of Florence by the River Arno with the serious damage to important library holdings made a tremendous impact on the whole library world.
9. Mr Nicholas Barker.
10. Dr Brian Enright, University Librarian, Newcastle upon Tyne.
11. National Library of Canada. *Conservation policies and activities in national libraries: report of a survey conducted by (Mrs Missy Hillman of) the National Library of Canada for the Conference of Directors of National Libraries*, typescript, Ottawa, 1982.
12. A 'Dissemination Seminar' to discuss the draft report of the project was held in Cambridge in September 1983 under the auspices of the British Library Research and Development Department. The papers, delivered for the most part by members of the Project Steering Committee, are incorporated in Appendix 4 to this report. In June 1983, the Library and Information Services Council (LISC) held a Seminar on Conservation in London, at which the Project Director gave an interim report on the project. Both seminars made significant

contributions to the present report and are referred to frequently within it.

13. The bulk of the extensive collection of mainly manuscript fragments from the Cairo Genizah was presented to the University Library by Solomon Schechter and Charles Taylor in 1898: it is administered by the Library's Taylor-Schechter Unit.

14. No 41, November 1982.

15. *British Standard 5454:1977* recommends temperature of 55.4 °F-64.4 °F (13 °C-18 °C) and relative humidity of 55%-65%.

16. *Factories Act, 1961* (9 and 10 Eliz.2.c.34) and *Offices, Shops and Railway Premises Act, 1963.*

17. Op cit, *Library and archives conservation*, vol 1, pp 39-43.

18. Stam, D H. *National preservation planning in the United Kingdom: an American perspective*, British Library R&D Report 5759, 1983, p 3.

19. Reichmann, F and Tharpe, J M. *Bibliographic control of microforms* (Sponsored by the Association of Research Libraries for the Office of Education) Westport, Conn, Greenwood Press, 1972.

20. National Reprographic Centre for documentation. NRCd Technical Evaluation Report, TER 73/4, Microfilm readers: a review of the trends, *NRCd Reprographics Quarterly*, vol 7, No 1, Winter 73/74, p 20.

21. Op cit, p 72.

22. Byrnes, M. Preservation of library materials: 1982. *Library Resources & Technical Services*, July/September, 1983, p 300.

23. *New Scientist*, 23/30 December, 1982, p 801.

24. National Library of Canada, *National Library News*, March-April 1982, vol 14, No 3-4, p 3.

25. Op cit, *Survey*, p i.

26. Cunha, op cit, vol 1, p 30 and p 9.

27. Quoted from the address given by the Director General of the Reference Division, Mr A Wilson.

28. Op cit, p 173.

29. Published until 1965-6 as University Grants Committee, *Returns from universities and university colleges*, thereafter by the Department of Education and Science, *Statistics of education*, vol 6, University Grants Committee, *Universities.*

30. See *Librarian's Annual Reports*, Manchester, University Library, 1965-80 and Ratcliffe, F W. Manchester University Library Bindery: a study of library efficiency and management, *Libri*, vol 20, 1970, pp 77-88.
31. Copyright Act, 1911, Section 15, and 1956.
32. *Eighteenth Century Short Title Catalogue*, Edited by R Alston, in progress.
33. University Grants Committee, *Capital provision for university libraries*, London, HMSO, 1976.
34. Op cit, p 2 and p 7.
35. National Library of Australia. *Managing the library preservation program*, typescript, Canberra, 1982, p 2.
36. Op cit, Quotations, vol II, p X; vol 1, p 12.
37. Op cit.
38. Op cit.
39. Gladstone, W E. On books and the housing of them, *The Nineteenth Century*, 27, 1890, p 385 and p 388.
40. Updike, D B. *Printing types, their history, forms and use.* Second edition, Cambridge, Mass, Harvard University Press, 1937, vol II, p 273.
41. Bailey, H S. *Interim report on book paper*. Washington, Council on Library Resources, 1981.
42. Mrs Gail Bradley is investigating the use of acid-free paper for the British Library.
43. Library of Congress, *National register of microform masters*, Washington, DC, Library of Congress, 1982, 2 vols.
44. Cf UK Group, International Institute for Conservation of Historic and Artistic Works. *Conservation in museums and galleries: a survey of facilities in the United Kingdom*, Portsmouth, Eyre & Spottiswoode, 1974, p 70, etc.
45. British Printing Industries Federation.

14 Glossary of conservation terms

Only those terms which occur in the report and which may not be familiar to all readers are included here. For the meaning of many terms found in binding generally the still valuable glossary appended to E A Clough's *Bookbinding for librarians*, published in London by the Association of Assistant Librarians in 1957, should be consulted. For conservation terms, Banks, Cunha and the Library of Congress Restoration Office among others, provide extensive and detailed further information.

Binding preparation – the binding preparation office where records of books despatched for conservation treatment, inside or outside the library, are made and where directions as to requirements are specified. After conservation, items are usually returned to this office.

Cased book – a book fastened into covers which are 'ready made' or part of a separate process.

Cleat sewn – a method of holding pages together, usually single leaves, by using a cleat sewer, which cuts grooves into the binding edges, and sews through them; they are then glued with a very flexible adhesive: advisable only in 'perfect' bindings.

Conservation – strictly, the repair work and binding carried out on items and of an essentially remedial nature. In present general usage 'conservation' and 'preservation' tend to be interchangeable. For example, the Canadian Survey talks of conservation policies and the Australian National Library of its preservation programme. There are numerous similar examples.

Conservation primer – an elementary manual of instruction on conservation measures.

Conservator – one capable of assessing the conservation requirements of materials in binding, technical and scientific terms and of carrying out the necessary work.

Craft binding – work incorporating the finest skills of the craftsman binder, usually completed entirely by hand.

Cut flush – the cutting 'flush' of the leaves and covers of a book in one operation after the boards have been attached (usually incorporating existing paper covers).

Deacidification – the neutralisation or elimination of acidity in paper, or other parts of a book, usually by some alkaline treatment.

Disaster planning – the planning of preparedness in a library to meet library emergencies, usually after fire or flood.

Finisher – the binder responsible for the lettering and decoration (i.e. the 'tooling') of the book on completion of the binding process.

Forwarder – the binder responsible for the construction of the book from the sewing to the finishing stages.

In-house bindery – a bindery located within or operated by the library.

'Lyfguarding' – a trade term for one method of self-adhesive, plastic covering used to strengthen paper-back books.

Mass deacidification – applied to methods currently being developed for the neutralisation of the acid in large numbers of books (up to 5,000), at one and the same time, through the application of scientific techniques in specially constructed vacuum chambers; still largely experimental and as yet not applied to older books.

Oversewing – passing the sewing thread through the edges of sections or groups of leaves, coming back over and repeating the process; also called 'whipping' and often found in machine sewing of books.

Paper-back – a book cased in paper covers glued to the back and often unsewn, i.e. 'perfect' bound.

Perfect binding – originally a trade term (of Sheridan Company, USA), but now of general application, for the glueing together of single leaves (i.e. without folds) at the binding edge to form a book, more usually with paper covers.

Phase box – a box constructed out of one piece of (acid-free) cardboard which is folded in a certain way to fit a book; devised by the Library of Congress Restoration Office as one 'phase' in their preservation programme.

Preservation – strictly, all the steps taken to protect materials, that is including conservation and restoration, but often used in reference to the treatment of materials on first entering the library; it is preventative rather than remedial. *See* Conservation.

Publishers' binding – refers to the binding applied to the whole edition or issue of a book. It is usually cased work, the cases normally being fitted in production of the book or on occasion (as in periodicals) provided by the publisher for fitting by the purchaser.

Restoration – restoring an item, either by rebinding or extensive repair, as near as possible to its original appearance, wherever possible using the original materials and seeking to retain its character, method of original construction, evidence of provenance, etc. It is the ultimate treatment in preservation, not favoured by all conservators.

Stationery binding – originally the production of ledgers, minute and account books, diaries, etc. but now by extension to loose-leaf, spiral and other forms of 'binding' found in stationers.

Trade bindery – usually a general bindery, outside an institution, undertaking all kinds of binding work, including craft binding, but more generally meeting commercial needs.

Wood pulp paper – paper using wood pulp as its principal raw material: it is potentially much more acidic (sulphuric acid) than paper based on rag materials.

APPENDIX I – THE QUESTIONNAIRES
CAMBRIDGE UNIVERSITY LIBRARY CONSERVATION PROJECT
Questionnaire

Preservation – Prevention of environmental damage to stock (shelving, handling, etc.).
Conservation – Repair work carried out on materials.

1. Name of Institution:

   Address and telephone number:

2. Estimated size of holdings – volumes or linear feet: _____

   Nature of holdings: _____

   Amount of use: Light ☐   Medium ☐   Heavy ☐

3. What proportion of your holdings is intended for permanent retention? _____

4. Do you have a written conservation/preservation policy?   Yes ☐   No ☐
   If so, *please enclose a copy*.

5. Do you have (a) An in-house bindery?
              (b) A specific conservation workshop?
              (c) If neither, repair facilities of any kind? _____

              (d) Access to facilities elsewhere? _____

6. Do you make use of outside firms?   All   Some   None
   (a) For your specialized repair work and/or craft binding?
   (b) For standard binding?

7. (a) How many general binders do you employ? _____
   (b) How many conservation technicians do you employ? _____

8. Is there a member of the library staff responsible for:

	Designation and grade	Approximate salary range
(a) Ordering conservation priorities:		
(b) Specifying repairs required on individual items:		

9. (a) What factors of internal library environment do you take into account as a means of preservation? _____

(b) Can you adjust storage conditions to meet preservation needs? (e.g. air-conditioning, dehumidifiers, etc)

Yes	No	Partial

(c) Do you monitor stack/repository conditions?

(d) What Relative Humidity range and temperature do you maintain in the stack area (on average)?

R/H	Temp.

(e) Do you have any systematic procedure for surveying or treating stock on the shelves?
If so, please specify:
Frequency of survey _____
Types of treatment _____

10. What kind of training have your newly qualified library staff received in the field of conservation/preservation? _____

11. Do you have any in-house programme in preservation awareness for library staff? Yes ☐ No ☐

If yes, please describe _____

12. Have you had recourse to existing scientific expertise for specific problems? Yes ☐ No ☐

From: University departments ☐   Industry ☐

Conservation laboratories ☐   Museums ☐

Other – please specify _____

13. Do you subscribe to any conservation journals?   Please list: _____

14. (a) What do you spend on conservation and binding per annum (approx)? _____
    (b) If carried out internally, please give estimate for:
    Staffing _____ and materials _____
    (c) How does this compare proportionately with your total acquisition budget? ___

15. (a) Do you use microforms as a means of preservation? Yes ☐ No ☐

If yes, please specify _____

		Yes	No
(b)	Do you have microfilming production facilities?		
(c)	Do you have special storage areas for microfilm?		

16. (a) Do you think there is a need for a national centre to advise on library conservation problems and to conduct research? _____

    (b) If such a centre were set up on a self-financing basis would you be prepared to pay for its services?   Yes ☐   No ☐

17. Do you have any difficulty in obtaining specific products for use in conservation repair? If so, please specify _____

18. Do you instruct library users in the handling of books and documents?   Yes ☐   No ☐

19. Do you have any further comments or specific problems concerning conservation/preservation?

20. Would you or a member of your staff be willing to be interviewed by the Conservation Project's Research Assistant within the next few months?   Yes ☐   No ☐

    If yes, which member of staff should she approach? _____

Signed by: _____

Position in organization: _____

(Please use additional sheets if necessary)

CAMBRIDGE UNIVERSITY LIBRARY
CONSERVATION PROJECT

Training Course Questionnaire

1. Name and address of Institution: _____

2. Name of Principal of Institution: _____

                                                                                                       Yes   No

3. Do you offer courses of any kind in Conservation/ Conservation awareness? ☐ ☐

    If so (a) Does it form part of another course? ☐ ☐
          (b) Constitute a course in itself: ☐ ☐

4. Is this course(s) aimed at educating

    (a) Professional librarians ☐
    (b) Binders ☐
    (c) Conservation technicians ☐
    (d) Other? _____

5. Name of person in charge of conservation course(s): _____

6. Type of course: Full-time ☐   day release ☐   undergraduate ☐
                              part-time ☐   evening ☐   postgraduate ☐

7. Duration of course: _____

8. Normal entrance requirements: _____

9. Maximum number of students admitted per course: _____

10. Brief description of course(s): _____

11. Please indicate the percentage of the course devoted to the following:

    i. Management/administration ☐

    ii. Practical (benchwork):   (a) binding ☐
                                        (b) archival repair ☐

    iii. Theory: (a) Need for conservation ☐
                     (b) environmental considerations ☐
                     (c) conservation techniques ☐
                     (d) history/bibliography ☐
                     (e) other _____

    iv. Scientific content: _____

    v.   Lectures by visiting specialists

        (a) Librarians ☐   (c) Scientists ☐

        (b) Archivists ☐   (d) Binders/con- ☐
                                        servators

        (e) Other: _____

12. Is any practical project or dissertation required? _____

13. Are students exposed to original materials? _____

14. Final qualification awarded: _____

    Is it granted on the basis of assessment ☐ examination ☐ or both ☐

15. Pass rate for course in 1982: _____

16. Number of teaching staff for this course(s): _____

17. Please state the specific training objectives of your course(s): _____

18. What other courses would you like to see available? _____

19. Comments:

                          Signed: _____

                Position in organisation: _____

                  (Please use additional sheets if necessary)

APPENDIX 2 – CONSERVATION POLICIES AND ACTIVITIES IN NATIONAL LIBRARIES: SYNOPSIS OF CANADIAN SURVEY[1]

SUMMARY

Profile of Conservation/Preservation Activities in the Average National Library.

Based on the reports received from 36 national libraries in the last year, it is possible to construct a profile of the preservation/conservation activities in national libraries.

National Perspective

The average country
does not:
a. have a national preservation policy for library materials;
b. have an active conservation/preservation program based on that policy.

does:
a. have at least one other agency which is involved in national conservation/preservation activities;
b. have between 1 and 10 institutions with in-house conservation facilities;
c. have less than 30 trained conservators in the country.

National Library's Leadership Role

The average national library
does not:
a. co-ordinate the national conservation/preservation program for library materials;
b. provide a conservation/preservation advisory service to other libraries in the country;
c. have an active program to raise conservation awareness;
d. provide central coordination for such conservation/preservation activities as standards, research, preservation microfilming, facsimile printings or videodisc;
e. maintain national register of microforms or facsimile reproductions;
f. undertake restoration and/or repair of materials for other libraries.

has not:
conducted a national survey of conservation/preservation needs, facilities or activities, nor does it plan to conduct such a survey;

---

[1] This is the summary of the report of a survey conducted by the National Library of Canada for the Conference of Directors of National Libraries, Ottawa, April 1982. It is reproduced here by kind permission of the Conference and the compiler, Mrs Missy Hillman.

does:

promote the training of practical conservators.

Internal Conservation/Preservation Activities

The average national library
does not:
a. have a written conservation/preservation policy for its own materials;
b. have a policy or plan for disasters or emergencies;
c. have special lighting considerations in its stack area;
d. have a separate department or branch for conservation activities.

has not:
a. conducted an in-house survey of its own preservation needs;

does:
a. have an active preservation/conservation program for library materials;
b. maintain environmentally controlled areas;
c. have special procedures or policies governing the use of materials in the library, on interlibrary loan and for exhibitions;
d. have programs for microfilming deteriorating or fragile materials;
e. carry out microfilming both in-house and by using outside firms;
f. select materials for conservation/preservation treatment both randomly and systematically;
g. support a variety of conservation/preservation activities both in-house and externally;
h. allocate less than 6 per cent of its operating budget to conservation/preservation;
i. have less than 20 persons employed for conservation/preservation activities;
j. locate the conservation unit administratively within an operational branch.

APPENDIX 3 - PAPERS SUBMITTED BY COMMITTEE MEMBERS TO THE PROJECT STEERING COMMITTEE, 7 APRIL 1982

The conservation needs and policies of libraries and record offices - Nicolas Barker, British Library Reference Division

Staff in libraries and other repositories of documents in the UK can be roughly divided into three groups:

1. Those who are aware of the needs presented by the material in their charge, who allocate funds both for its preservation and conservation, and who have their own directly employed staff engaged on the latter.
2. Those who are aware of the needs, and allocate funds, but do not have their own conservation resources.
3. Those who are simply aware of the needs, but have no means of meeting them.

There are still some library staff who are simply unaware that the problem exists, but even here ignorance is relative rather than total, and the general increase of interest and awareness in conservation overall is making itself more and more felt in libraries.

The first class of repositories is still relatively small: the copyright libraries, PRO and IOLR, and a few major university libraries, possess their own conservation resources. They vary in size from the British Library with about 150 employed to small workshops. None of them is anything like equal to the demands made by the quantity of material in need of conservation. The quality of treatment varies considerably, and probably only Trinity College Dublin would generally be regarded as possessing a workshop capable of the highest standards of work. Most of the workshops and binderies have just grown from an ordinary bindery, and the degree and nature of the conservation skills added to simple binding reflect the needs and attitudes of the different institutions over a period of time. Awareness of modern methods, feeling for aesthetic and historic needs, and just plain competence vary considerably. It is worth drawing a particular distinction between record offices and libraries: record office staff have always regarded physical preservation of their material as a primary and integral part of their job (many archivists are capable of elementary conservation procedures); library staff by tradition regard conservation as incidental and not part of a librarian's job, rather a binder's.

So much for conservation work done inside libraries. Many more libraries bestow funds (their own or raised elsewhere) on conservational binding, done off the premises by individual craftsmen or larger firms. These links provide a wide range of skills and costs. Generally speaking, larger libraries tend to deal with larger firms and smaller with individual craftsmen, though the largest library may employ a specialist for a particular job and some large firms deal with individual clients for a single book. The danger of 'out-housing' conservation is that it leads to the belief that it is not an 'in-house' job, which may lead to the neglect of elementary procedures like cleaning and furbishing. This is a problem that will be considered further later. The range of libraries runs from major publicly funded institutional repositories, to private institutional libraries, to private libraries (some of them as large and historically important as any institutional library), to possessors (public or private) of a single book or document. Ecclesiastical foundations, particularly cathedrals, present special problems, as do institutions whose function has changed with time (e.g. old private subscription libraries, mechanics' institutes and learned societies). Private collections are perhaps the largest problem of all.

The quality of treatment available also varies. The largest firms generally provide a standard service which guarantees a respectable minimum level of workmanship but excludes the upper range of skills (such as the treatment of unstable coloured pigments on paper, or the treatment of badly damaged vellum). The number of conservators who are capable of these skills (adding to them the now necessary competence in chemistry) is still far smaller than the market, even inadequately funded as it is, requires. Besides these there are a range of smaller firms and individual craftsmen of varying skills: some are capable of elementary paper conservation, others of binding only; some know how to strengthen a weakened book-structure without seriously disturbing it, others provide the appearance without any real support. All of them together are still insufficient for the demand.

If funding the physical repair of documents and books, the 'above the line' element in the conservation budget, is inadequate, 'below the line' expenditure, on the environment in which material is kept, is even less adequate, though it is or ought to be as large or larger. There is even less expertise available in this field than in manual conservation, yet the overall preservation of material depends on it. The greater amount of documents and books that are in reasonable condition will not remain so unless conditions of storage and usage are good. This depends upon setting standards for the control of temperature and humidity, control of environmental pollution, exposure to light, shelving and storage, cleaning and furbishing (both mechanical and human) and above all use. No such standards are applied or even widely known. Use in turn requires an understanding of users' needs, which may in turn decree limitation or substitution. Again, precedents are hard to find and coordination is rudimentary.

If the problems of the libraries and record repositories that have funds are extended to those that have none, all the problems referred to above are merely multiplied many times. This factor accentuates a general latent problem: what criterion is to be applied for the preservation of material? Given resources which will (even if vastly increased) remain inadequate, how is one to ensure that they are properly deployed, and that what needs preservation is properly kept and if necessary repaired? And how is one to justify the choice of what will not be so treated and will have a measurable and decreasing life-span? No library has a preservation *policy*, properly based on an understanding of, and balance between, these factors.

Among all the problems of lack of funds, inadequate accommodation, damaged material and shortage of conservators and binders, the overall problem of a preservation policy, which must vary from institution to institution (and person to person), is the greatest. It requires a knowledge of the archaeological structure of the material, a view of its textual or social importance, an understanding of the use to which it has been, is being and will be put, and a grasp of the purpose of the repository as a whole.

Archivists have a better record than librarians in concern for physical conservation, but neither has paid as much attention to the archaeological, as opposed to evidential, value of collections or individual pieces. Conservators and binders are valuable adjuncts to decisions of this sort, and should be partners to them, but they cannot be expected to take them single-handed, with an imperfect knowledge of all the considerations required. Left alone, they may do the wrong thing, or at least more than the real circumstances warrant. Equally, owners, institutional and private, need advice if they are to dispose of limited funds to the best advantage.

A nationally coordinated preservation policy can only be achieved if four immediate needs are satisfied:

1. The primary need is for training which would equip librarians and others to understand these problems and take these decisions.
2. There is a need for more trained technical staff: more fully competent conservators, binders who understand how little as well as how much to do, furbishers who can undertake a limited range of elementary procedures reliably.
3. There is a crying need for more money to support these activities, and to overcome overall problems of environment and use.
4. There is a need for advice, which might be supplied by a national inspectorate, rather on the French model.

Without some progress on all these fronts – and the most elementary need of all is training, without which a start cannot be made – no policy can be adequately formulated or its needs met.

Rare book conservation - Nicholas Pickwoad, Conservator and Institute of Paper Preservation, Norwich

Among the many shortages in the field of book conservation, one of the most serious, because least easy to correct, is that of trained binders able to understand and treat sympathetically those books kept in the Rare Book or Special Collection categories in libraries. These binders, who can usefully be described as conservation binders, need an extremely wide range of technical skills, but beyond that they must also be well versed in the history and theory of binding structures, must be aware of the various uses to which books may be put, and must be familiar with the types of information sought and used by researchers. In the absence of librarians with a thorough knowledge of conservation, they must also be able to give accurate information on the possibilities and consequences, practical and historical, of any action taken, and its advisability. Whilst the final responsibility must always rest with the librarian, the conservator should have an established place in the decision making processes whenever matters concerning the physical state of the books are discussed. Their advice should be sought at an early date on matters concerning exhibition, new library stacks, etc. If the library world wants to be able to make use of intelligent conservators, and not mere technicians, they must build an acceptance of the trained conservator's contribution into his role within a library.

On a more detailed level, the fact that the book conservator is normally the only person to see the structural detail of the book he works on places an historical responsibility on the conservator which he must be equipped to meet. Few librarians have the training or knowledge to recognise the importance, potential or actual, of such physical detail, nor, in most cases the opportunity. Therefore, historical knowledge and sensitivity, and awareness of the book as an object as well as a work of reference is crucial. The preservation of the historical as well as the bibliographical integrity of many Special Collection books is necessary if we are to preserve an important aspect of our history. To this end, the conservator needs to know, and to be able to assert, what he cannot do as well as what he can. A book rebound may be an historical object destroyed, however skillfully the work is carried out. Decisions in this area can only be reached by both the librarian and the conservation binder.

Historical and bibliographical training in current bookbinding courses, where it exists at all, is totally inadequate. The consequences of repair work as being something not necessarily desirable are scarcely touched on. If binders do not understand why they are doing what they are trained to do, bad work will result, and if they do not understand wherein the interest of the book lies, they can easily destroy it. The only solution to this problem is to restructure, or, if necessary, totally redesign the existing courses to accommodate the teaching required.

As important is the need to include in the librarian's training a comprehensive instruction in the possibilities and theory of conservation. This is particularly important for those librarians who will be working in institutions which do not have established conservation facilities, and where conservation work is, as a result, contracted out. In these circumstances, a librarian who is unable to distinguish between good and bad practice in the field of book conservation will be severely handicapped when selecting binders for individual jobs. In addition, in view of the fact that there are many inadequately trained binders available to the librarian, it is essential that the librarian is able to set the required standards when commissioning work. Increased knowledge and awareness in this area on the part of the librarian is likely to be the most effective way of raising standards which are frequently very low. If a Cathedral librarian is still prepared to consider the contemporary calf binding on a first edition of Donne's poems too drab, and have it replaced in modern gold tooled morocco, as happened within the last three years, there is an obvious need for education. If librarians claim the final responsibility, they must be in a position to make informed decisions, and the training of librarians is as crucial as that of conservators. Each must be able to comprehend the work, demands and limitations of the other.

In my experience, many librarians are ignorant of even the most basic elements of book care, let alone book conservation, and handle books in a way which helps to destroy them. All too often, rare books are made to conform to library practices, rather than vice-versa. One way to an improvement in this situation is the appointment of a conservation administrator, but the question remains, where is he to get his training? He must have a sophisticated knowledge of the problems involved in conservation, and this is not something that can be picked up in a week or two of taking the job. The combined conservation and conservation administration course at Columbia University in New York is an attempt to face up to this problem, but has no parallel over here. Conservation must not be regarded as an optional extra to library training, but as fundamental to it. Equally, the trained conservator should not have to force his way into the librarian's awareness.

Scope of the conservation project

Conservation is inevitably concerned with quality, and I cannot see that a survey carried out without regard to quality will have any great value. It is not enough simply to read the syllabus supplied by a training course to know whether the course itself is in any way adequate. Most syllabuses will give an impression of a comprehensive and effective course, even though the course itself may fall short of its promises in important respects. An investigation of the quality of what is taught might give a very different impression. Similarly, a workshop may contain sophisticated equipment and offer sophisticated treatments, but the results may still be unacceptable. If we are to assess the national capability in book conservation, we cannot avoid some attempt to include qualitative judgments. Among the areas of immediate interest are the following:

1. Handling of books. Are the staff in the library instructed in the correct and safe ways of moving books from stack to reading room and back? Is the library equipment adequate for the job?

2. Definition of levels of conservation. Are the library staff who make decisions about conservation aware of the different levels of work available in conservation workshops and where to apply them?

3. Existing systems for grading and commissioning work. Do libraries have adequate means for sorting books for treatment and ensuring that correct treatments are carried out?

4. 'The museum of the book'. Is there an awareness of the importance of books in an archaeological sense and of the dangers to this importance from repair?

5. The role of the conservator. What place does the conservator have within the hierarchy of the library and is he involved in decisions affecting the physical well-being of the books?

6. Qualifications of the staff. Are the staff who are given the responsibility for overseeing conservation work adequately trained to carry out this task? What qualifications, if any, are required?

The scientific aspects of conservation: the Cambridge 1980 Conference - F W Ratcliffe, Project Director, Cambridge University Library

In 1980 an international conference on the conservation of library and archive materials and the graphic arts was held at Cambridge, England. It was sponsored jointly by the Society of Archivists and the Institute of Paper Conservation. The abstracts and preprints of the papers appeared under the title *Conservation of library and archive materials and the graphic arts*. They make an important up-to-date contribution to the scientific aspects of conservation, internationally and in the UK. They also provide some insight into the scholarly level of the scientific approach. This brief paper refers almost entirely to that publication, presenting as it does one of the most recent accounts of the problems in this area of library and archive management.

The section on 'Scientific development in paper conservation' is of interest for more than the content of the papers. It throws some light on to the credentials and background of the contributors. From Canada, four conservators presented highly scientific papers on the characterisation of enzymes for use in paper conservation. Three of the four came from the Department of Conservation Processes Research of the Canadian Conservation Institute and are highly qualified research chemists. The fourth, also a scientist, was formerly head of the Processes Research Department and is now Acting Chief of Regional Services of the Canadian Conservation Institute.

From West Germany there were four representatives. Two were from the Department of Cellulose and Paper Chemistry of the Institute for Macromolecular Chemistry at the Technical University of Darmstadt, one of them having been previously employed by the Cellulose and Paper Department of the National Research Centre, Cairo. Each approached conservation from a highly scientific base, that is, purely as scientists. The other two German contributors were the Professor in Paper Converting, Paper Chemistry and Paper Coating in the Technological University of Munich, and the Director of the Institute for Book and Manuscript Restoration in the Bavarian State Library, Munich. The latter has a postgraduate qualification in academic librarianship, but both are highly qualified in science, operating from science-based departments. All four German contributions were pitched at a high scientific level.

The contributions in this section from the UK were all from the Conservation Section of the Bodleian. One graduated in Chemistry and pursued research in that field and from 1972-80 was a College Assistant Librarian. The second is a biochemist who researched in that subject until

1979. The third trained initially in Paris as a book-binder. Their subject was the treatment of enzymes in partially non-aqueous media. Of the contributions in this section dealing with scientific developments, that of the Bodleian was the one most easily comprehensible to the librarian with little or no scientific background, that is, not requiring specific scientific knowledge in order to comprehend it.

The absence of contributions from university science departments or any national conservation institution in the UK is significant. Given the nature of the contributions from overseas it might have been expected that some representative, for example, from the Department of Polymer and Fibre Science at UMIST or from the Chemical Laboratory of an industrial concern would have made a contribution. The fact that they did not suggests perhaps a somewhat different relationship of science with conservation in the UK to that found elsewhere, an approach at a different scholarly level, at least as far as conservation in libraries is concerned.

Such a conclusion based on this evidence alone might be thought premature not to say unwarranted, but there is support for it elsewhere in the same publication. The section dealing with training is particularly instructive. The educational opportunities in the UK are limited, except at a rather basic level, and training is especially short on any scientific input when compared with schemes in operation overseas. The in-service training scheme for archivists offered by the Society of Archivists includes the chemical aspects of conservation as part of a one-week course. The Camberwell School of Art and Crafts now offers BA degrees, validated by the Council of National Academic Awards (CNAA), but it is still heavily committed to courses dependent on manual dexterity. Entry to book-binding and paper conservation courses depends on minimal O-level attainments. The level of the CNAA degree courses must obviously be much higher but it would be difficult to compare their scientific component with the courses in a university science department. Seen in the context of the courses described in Spain, the USA and Denmark, in the same section on training, a very different approach to conservation training, especially in terms of science, emerges for the UK. At no point is entry envisaged at the same level of training as that provided in these countries.

This is not to imply that no scientific expertise exists in the UK in the field of conservation. A glance at the staff list of the Department of Polymer and Fibre Science at UMIST, which includes among its chairs one in Paper Science, is sufficient to disprove that. Moreover, from the publication under discussion, it can be noted that it is (or was) possible to take a BSc (Leather Science) at Leeds University and that such a graduate is head of the Science Department of the National Leathersellers' Centre in Northampton; that the Head of the Biology Department of the British

Leather Manufacturers' Research Association also at Northampton is a scientist; that the British Museum employs highly trained scientists in its Department of Conservation and Technical Services. What seems to be missing is a coordinated national approach to scientific conservation needs, an awareness in scientific scholarship of the scientific implications for conservation in the world of printed books and manuscripts and, in professional librarianship, of the opportunities which already exist outside the few recognised channels. The current advertisement for a Head of Conservation in the National Library of Scotland requires 'sound knowledge of practical experience of the chemistry of library materials and related conservation problems, including those posed by the environment'. No traditional library or technical craft training channels can meet such requirements at present in the UK; only training based on long experience of the problems themselves can provide such a person.

The reference to the British Museum's Department of Conservation and Technical Services and its participation in the Cambridge Conference underlines the fact that a considerable body of relevant expertise exists outside libraries and record offices. Moreover, the existence of the United Kingdom Institute for Conservation of Historic and Artistic Works, originally part of but now affiliated to the International Institute, indicates that it exists in an organised form both at national and international levels. The United Kingdom Institute publishes *Conservation News* and its own journal *The Conservator*. Although obviously weighted in directions of little application to libraries, such as archaeology or sculpture, many of its activities and techniques are of direct interest and relevance to the conservation problems of libraries and record offices. There is a certain amount of obvious common ground.

It would seem, therefore, expedient to assess the areas for cooperation and coordination offered by this essentially museum-based institute and other similar bodies. There is evidence of a scientific contribution to conservation at a high scholarly level of a kind not found in the library field in any coordinated way in the UK. There are certain to be similar lessons in the conservation activities of such bodies as the Museums' Association or the Association of British Picture Restorers. The training programmes and recruitment policies of such organisations may well shed interesting light on their scientific component and provide pointers for libraries to the way forward.

It is highly desirable, therefore, to have an assessment of all the conservation activities which may impinge on document conservation, if only in the most general way. Equally important is to establish exactly what specific provision already exists, not by pointing yet again to the Camberwell School, the Society of Archivists and the more widely known bodies, but in identifying all the relevant courses which are available. There must be some assessment of the element of conservation in postgraduate library courses and some idea of the scientific content of conservation training courses already operating under a variety of different auspices. At the moment there is but a vague awareness of what may be available, of who is doing what, without any coordinated approach to standards of training or conservation entry requirements. The potential for conservation, training and research, to be found in universities, polytechnics and industry has to be assessed. University department staff and others in higher education with expertise relevant to conservation scientific training may well be completely ignorant of library need and are likely to respond favourably, especially in these difficult financial times, if approached. Much the same must be true of industrial concerns in this field. Any proposal for a national policy on conservation must relate the need for a sound scientific base to the more traditional technical skills and recognise the implications for the education of professional librarians. It must be fully aware of the facilities and opportunities which already exist, inside or outside the world of libraries, archives and record offices.

The problems of surveying the 'state of the art' in regard to the conservation of library materials - D Thomas, Public Record Officer, London

The 'state of the art' in many libraries can be demonstrated by looking at my own institution. The Public Record Office (PRO) has a large, trained staff for the conservation of records and has facilities and equipment to fumigate, repair, laminate and deacidify paper and to repair parchment. Archival binding can be undertaken, as can work on prints, maps, photographs and other materials. The PRO also has a library of historical, topographical, legal and archival works. When library books are in need of repair, they are sent off to commercial binders who are able to do no more than resewing and replacing the boards and covers.

The conservation of records, prints and drawings has now far outrun the skills of print trade binders. There is also a psychological difference: archivists are used to employing conservationists and tend to assume that records will need conservation treatment. Librarians are used to employing binders and tend to assume that binding is all that is required.

Although the idea of conservation has been accepted by archivists, there is no general agreement as to which techniques are the best. There is much disagreement as to the most suitable method of deacidification, how to repair paper and which materials are the most suitable for conservation. There is a wide divergence of views as to the best methods of repairing parchment. Methods advocated include sewing, patching with silk and paper, patching with parchment, the use of natural sausage skin casing, goldbeaters' skin or the swim bladder of a fish.

In this situation, the best that can be done is to look at those areas in which there is agreement in an effort to discover how far libraries and binderies are following the practices of archive and print and drawing conservationists. Enquiries should be made as to how far binderies have the skills and equipment for the following practices and how far librarians insist that the practices be carried out.

A. Fumigation

Any bindery involved in conservation should have safe facilities for the destruction of mould and insect infestations by the use of fumigation. It is probable that binderies will use thymol and paradichlorobenzene, but other methods may be in use. An attempt should be made to discover which binderies and libraries have facilities for fumigation and what facilities they have.

B. *Deacidification*

The presence or absence of facilities for deacidification is the best test of whether or not a bindery is using conservation techniques. Deacidification is vital for many book papers. Acceptable techniques vary widely. The best methods are aqueous, involving immersion in alkaline solutions. Other methods include the use of gaseous or vapour deacidification or the application of deacidification solutions by spray or brush. It would be useful to know whether institutions have facilities for pH testing and for deacidification and what criteria are used to decide whether paper should be deacidified.

C. *Paper repair*

The processes involved here are:

1. Cleaning paper by aqueous or dry methods.
2. Traditional or 'Bodleian' repair: a method of paper repair requiring high levels of skills. This technique has been tested over many years and is 100% safe and reliable. It is expensive and consequently may be reserved for the most valuable papers.
3. Lamination: the simple sandwiching of paper between two sheets of transparent tissue. The technique is easy to apply and needs only semi-skilled staff. It has only been in use for about 20 years and so may not be felt suitable for the most valuable books. It can produce an unattractive look and feel to a document.
4. 'Florentine' repair: the technique of in-filling missing areas of paper with a repair which is held in place by laminating tissue. This method requires only semi-skilled staff and has the great advantage of producing a repair of even thickness. It has the disadvantages of lamination.
5. Paper pulp repair: the in-filling of missing areas with fibres in the form of paper pulp which is either applied manually or in a 'leaf caster'. This is a comparatively new method which appears to have considerable potential for the conservation of books.

An attempt to find out which binderies have the facilities or staff for these repair methods and what criteria are employed in choosing repair techniques to be used should be made.

D. *Conservation materials*

There is much concern amongst archive conservationists to use the most suitable materials, that is materials which will not harm the records to which they are applied. To a certain extent, the choice of materials is a matter for judgment by the conservationist, but attempts have been made to establish scientific criteria. It is not known whether librarians and binders are aware of the need to use the most suitable materials. Attempts should be made to discover the criteria on which materials are selected.

E.   Binding materials

A considerable amount of information is now available as to the longevity of various sorts of leather used in book binding. It is generally agreed that untanned skins such as vellum, mineral tanned skins and skins tanned with sumac survive better than skins tanned in other ways. It would be worth assessing whether librarians and binders are aware of and use such information.

F.   Negative responses

It is vitally important to chart areas of ignorance and areas in which libraries and binderies have fallen behind archive and prints and drawings conservationists.

Microforms for conservation needs - M L Turner, The Bodleian Library, Oxford

If it is agreed that even if we were all given unlimited resources for skilled conservators, binders and materials, the high - and ever rising - costs of physical treatment make the increasing use of microforms for purely conservation reasons more and more attractive. For an ever increasing amount of material it is cheaper to provide a microform alternative than to attempt any conservation treatment of the original. Given these circumstances it would be advantageous to librarians and conservation administrators, who may not have the time to plough through the ever growing and increasingly technical literature, if the project stimulated some debate on the following:

1. One of the basic concerns is the necessity of all librarians to be clear as to the nature of their collections - which parts it is necessary to preserve, and which can be used up or abandoned and under what circumstances. A clear policy on these matters is essential to all libraries, but it will be exceedingly important to any programme of providing microforms for conservation reasons. Incidentally, it will also be necessary for the librarian to be clear, even within the more limited area of microform materials themselves, which items can be used to extinction and which must be of archival quality, treated as archival materials, and preserved for the future.

2. Having made the choice of which materials it is desirable to supply in microform and for what reasons, librarians will wish to be informed in simple terms as to the technical possibilities available to them, the relative costs, advantages and disadvantages of the various forms, the readers and printers that those forms will require. A similar short guide will be needed in regard to the differing storage requirements of the various forms and qualities of materials (e.g. as between silver halide and diazo or vesicular film).
   Where standards have already been agreed and laid down (e.g. Library of Congress's *Specifications for microfilming manuscripts*; or, the American National Standards Institute's *American practice for storage of processed safety photographic film*; or, the British Standards Institution's *Recommendations for the processing and storage of silver gelatin-type microfilm*), librarians need to know which can be recommended.

3. It is desirable to have a brief outline for the guidance of those required to carry out bibliographical searches for commercially available microforms or for the existence of archival negatives: also some guidance as to the amount of search that is economically realistic in relation to the cost of various categories of material. It would be

foolish to spend more on such a search than it would cost to generate a new item. The sort of 'brief outline' I had in mind would be similar to that supplied for American librarians by Pamela Darling in 1974, *Locating materials in microform*.

4. Related to this question of bibliographical search should be some inquiry into whether or not the bibliographical control of such material in the UK is adequate, and if not then how could it be improved. Would there be any mileage in contemplating a UK version of the *National register of microform masters*, or, would there be advantages in some central agency for information on the availability of microforms and archival negatives, and if so how should the setting up of such an agency be approached?

5. The ever increasing amount of conservation surveying that will be done in future years will inevitably draw attention to suitable materials for conservation filming. Consideration should be given to the question of the advantages to be gained by the creation of some central collecting point or clearing house for such information. Should such a centre be institutionally based or taken on by a commercial enterprise? There are advantages to microform publishers in having access to such information.

6. Better bibliographical control in this area should lead to a more rationalised approach to filming, and the prospects of cooperation between libraries and groups of libraries should be explored. In this context a certain amount of American experience should be investigated. There are several cooperative ventures in joint programmes of conservation filming in North America (e.g. Stanford and certain other Californian libraries have been working a joint scheme for several years).

7. Cooperation in other fields, where heavy capital expenditure may be expected, should be explored. The storage requirements for archival negatives are clearly expensive to provide, and some joint venture in providing a central storage facility, with perhaps an adjoining processing laboratory for the production of copies, might be worth considering.

8. Some general discussion is required as to the subsequent ramifications of the much greater use of microforms for conservation reasons; the necessity of a political will in directing readers to the use of microforms rather than the originals, the implications to accessions and cataloguing departments in doing this, the logistics involved within the library in introducing such a policy, etc. Much of this will be determined by the nature and circumstances of the particular library, but it should not be overlooked.

9. Finally, it may be considered necessary to provide some of the basic arguments in favour of the conservation advantages of microforms which many of us may take for granted. Any reasonable programme in any of our major libraries is certainly going to mean a massive switch of resources over the next few years – but then so will any commitment to conservation.

APPENDIX 4 - PAPERS READ AT THE CAMBRIDGE DISSEMINATION SEMINAR, 22 SEPTEMBER 1983

Priorities and planning: an approach to policy and strategy
Nicolas Barker, British Library Reference Division

Almost all libraries face, even if they do not know or acknowledge it, some problem in preservation. As the project report[1] points out, even a library whose avowed policy is to keep nothing beyond a term of contemporary readers' needs may find its stock in danger, due to unexpectedly heavy use or inadequate manufacture, before its function is exhausted. What next? Buy another copy (if one is still available), or repair the one you have? Already, the problem exists. Or it may be thrust on a library by other needs than its own: a book bought for immediate use that has lain fallow since may be found to have an importance outside the library's own constituency, an importance that demands its preservation. What do you do now? Sell it and transfer the responsibility elsewhere, or keep it and accept the responsibility, and the change in the library's status that that implies?

All these questions imply *choice*, the duty to choose between alternatives, which is the prime element in the formation of a library's preservation plan. Now it would be relatively easy if the questions presented themselves neatly in the sort of form I have just suggested. But it is not so simple. First, decisions about individual books cannot be taken in isolation: a book in a library is not just a book, but part of the whole library; the needs of the whole complicate a decision about the part. Secondly, few libraries do in fact operate a policy of total obsolescence. Whether by historic accident or choice, keeping is part of any library's function. Measuring contemporary need against duty to its heritage, not to say duty to posterity, is a constant feature of the librarian's task. It is never quite the same from day to day, or book to book.

But, however unsought, however variable with changing circumstances, choice is the vital element in preservation. All libraries have more to preserve than resources for preservation. But you cannot turn your back on the past, concentrate on new acquisitions, and 'let the back stock look after itself'. It won't. In terms of wasted space and dirt alone, it forces recognition on the library management. Nor can you operate a random system, by spending what you can afford on the first books that come to hand (or a reader complains about), or the oldest books, or the most valuable - if they just go back to join their less fortunate mates, on the shelves on which they originally came to grief, they will soon come to grief again.

---

[1] A draft version of the project report was circulated to those attending the Dissemination Seminar for information and discussion. References to the 'report' in Appendix 4 relate to that but are valid also for the published version.

So, choosing what to keep and in what order – what has first claim and what must be postponed – is the first duty. Choice must be extended to the entire stock, even to the latest arrived paperback. Choice, in turn, forces other difficult decisions. Is the present to be given priority over the past – or the future? What are the real needs of readers? Should these books, which are easy to repair, be preferred to those whose treatment is harder or dubiously possible?

Conditions of storage and environmental considerations are other factors. So are the forms in which readers want the material and the alternative methods of treatment available – I will come to these alternatives in a moment.

It all seems very complex and difficult, but all these factors have to be weighed and a policy established, for the library as a whole and for each individual item in it. Taken in the abstract, it may seem impossibly hard, but the real factors in each individual case convert the problem from algebra to mere arithmetic. Let me give you an example. Some years ago, I was consulted by a cathedral library about its conservation problems, which ranged from some famous mediaeval manuscripts, cockled and with the top edges scorched and corroded from the molten lead that poured on them when the roof was burnt in 1621, to a unique collection of pamphlets on 19th-century church history – *Septem Contra Christi*, the first Vatican congress, even pastoral charges from the Bishop of Ajaccio to his clergy – now beginning to decay. What was to be done first? Well, the mediaeval manuscripts were obviously the most *important* – yet, they had not suffered more damage since 1621 nor were likely to, whereas the pamphlets were visibly in urgent need of treatment. Furthermore, skilled conservators capable of handling the manuscripts are few and busy, while the pamphlets could be safely entrusted to a large conservation binding firm. In any case, it was not a question of all or nothing, the manuscripts or the pamphlets. The right decision was to allocate so much time and money to each, taking due account of value (not just in cash terms), urgency and available resources, human and financial. If you get down to it like this, choice is always possible, if never easy.

What, then, are the alternatives open to a librarian making such a choice? At the outset, there is the problem of preservation and conservation: how much of your resources do you devote to preventing or slowing down decay, and how much to repairing what has already decayed? This is an important crux, unfamiliar because the resources for preservation are often not distinct: environmental control is not separated from the heating bill; shelving is left to the architect or seen as a problem of access rather than preservation. On the other hand, it is futile to send books back to rickety shelves beneath a leaky roof with hot pipes all around, and windows exposing them to direct sunlight. Most libraries, as the report shows, have inadequate control of such matters: their first need is to set aside some part of the budget to putting them right.

Putting aside the degree of priority to be set on each of these elements (which are bound to vary with the individual circumstances of every library), let us now consider the alternatives for treatment of the books themselves. The first is to distinguish between the needs imposed by use of the *physical form* of the book and its *informational content*. There is an uncomfortable tendency now to equate these with museum-type preservation on the one hand, and on the other preservation in microform or some other alternative to the book, which may or may not be retained. This is not the place to embark on argument about the obsolescence or otherwise of the book: it is important, however, to make it clear that conservation is not the conversion of books into museum objects, and that alternative methods of preserving the informational content, whether in microform, optical disk or whatever other mode of digital storage and display the future holds, are better used in coexistence with the book, written or printed.

In this context, conservation of the physical form of books can be seen not as a unique process, but a whole series of alternatives in a spectrum that reaches from first binding to cathode-ray tube display. As the report indicates there is a great demand for first binding, from an economic process for securing books that have started life in a cut-back – I will not call it perfect – binding, to the classical structure, sewn on to cords drawn into boards covered with leather and appropriately finished. (I should mention, in parenthesis, that leather, out of favour due to cost and the poor resistance of new skins to modern environmental problems, is due for a revival, thanks to the successful development by the British Leather Manufacturers Research Association of a treatment which is proof against atmospheric pollution and other hazards.) There is an even greater need for conservators and craftsmen capable of treating paper and binding structures with a sound historic understanding of both. So much damage has been done in the past by well-meaning attempts to do the best (too often equivalent to the most) for a book, where a historic sense allied to manual skill would have suggested a more restrained approach.

At the same time, there are many books which need to be repaired and strengthened for use, as well as others which genuinely deserve 'museum' preservation. I foresee that the range of alternative treatments, from the fully fitted permanent box to temporary or 'phase' boxes, for the latter purpose will expand greatly in the future, and with it the librarian's choice of options. All this will dictate a much more flexible attitude to the concept of use. At the moment, books are either used or not used. If not used, they are all too apt to be locked away in safes or exhibition cases and deprived of their main function. If destined for use, current orthodoxy demands that they shall be fit for the heaviest and most insensitive handling they can possibly suffer. There is a need here for an imaginative and outgoing attitude to users: don't build dugouts and wait for the heavy artillery bombardment, but go out and meet the invasion half-way, with an olive branch rather than a rocket.

Here alternative methods of making information available will assume a new importance. Gone (I hope) are the days when microfilming was a licence to destroy the original. The right approach will take two objectives: first, to select material which will be *easier* (or at least as easy) to consult in an alternative form, e.g. modern statistical compilations or newspapers, where reference rather than consecutive reading is required; and secondly to use the alternative with access to the original. There will be useful side-effects in both cases: in the first, it will gradually accustom readers to the 'new technology' in which material will increasingly be originally presented; secondly, it will add point to the need that I have just mentioned to encourage a variety of uses, informed by understanding of the different structures. 'New technology' has much to offer the reader if it can be presented in an obviously useful form, and not identified with the restrictions on use that bring out the Luddite in all of us. Manuscripts and even printed books are not always easy to read. New devices exist for making erased or obliterated writing legible, and of reading words lost in the back of tightly bound volumes. Even simple magnification equipment is a neglected asset. Judicious presentation of these advantages can make 'new technology', in the odious modern phrase, 'user friendly'.

All these alternatives may be variously tempting or repulsive, but as far as the librarian, gloomily surveying the shelves of decrepit old books and flimsy new ones, is concerned, they all have one thing in common: they cost money. True, some money may be saved by avoiding unnecessary rebinding, but it is hard to see how any sort of new technology can save money except in a future well off the end of the longest budget projection. If all goes well, if the choices are accurately assessed, the right alternatives chosen, and a sound preservation policy established and implemented – if all this goes well, the current budget (unlikely to be increased in today's conditions) may go a little further, do a bit better. It will, however, take many more librarian-hours and whatever unit you measure librarian's energy and thought in, and, with all that, the impact on the current conservation backlog will be hardly visible even to the eye of faith. It is a depressing prospect.

Is there no hope of a real saving? Well, there is one, although it is still some way off. The report notes the activity in the Western hemisphere in evolving processes for bulk deacidification, which has so far not been taken up in

Europe. There are technological reasons for this, but behind this apparent hesitation is an important difference. Acid, acquired in the paper-making process or absorbed from the polluted atmosphere, is an important agent in the rapid decay of modern paper but it is not the only one: the imperfect chemical structure of lignin, an indissoluble component of the cellulosic pulp made from timber, has an equally damaging effect. A research project financed by the British Library Reference Division has been exploring the possibility of graft copolymerisation of certain monomers in the vapour phase, a system which offers a permanent support (and stable deacidification) for lignin-degraded papers. It will be some time before it can be established whether such a process can be devised and then scaled up, for the mass treatment of books. The present indications are that it can be done: if it can, it deserves the warmest encouragement from librarians, because the savings will be immediate. The decay of newspapers and an increasing number of books made from inferior wood-pulp paper is not in the remote future: it is happening now. If, at insignificant cost (as is likely to be the case), a whole mass of material, which needs at present to be deacidified and encapsulated or laminated, can be preserved without other treatment, the real cost of preservation of a growing amount of new material will be substantially reduced.

But with every advantage that can be extracted by cash or hard work from the available resources, no library can hope to solve its own problems single-handed. This brings me to my final point: cooperation. There are many areas in which cooperative action can reduce the overall preservation problem. The most obvious is acquisition. Not every library that acquires a copy of the same book has an equal duty to preserve it at all costs. Joint action then, to determine which libraries have an archival responsibility to preserve certain classes of material is vital. Progress will, inevitably, be slow, but that should not deter us from making a start. Even if no commensurate indication of the total saved by dividing the responsibility for preservation can be achieved, it is worthwhile merely in terms of saving or deflecting reader use and several other areas of preservation.

Other similar advantages that would accrue come from such projects as the proposed National Register of Microfilms which would prevent the national damage due to repeated filming of books of which a microfilm already exists. There is equal need for cooperation on planning for disasters, where one library may have advantages and equipment which could easily be put at the disposal of other libraries. It all very much depends on an efficient human communication system, and here there are signs that the need for an exchange of information and pooling of resources has brought it about. Other instances would be the Mass Paper Support system (once it gets off the ground) and training. The importance of the latter has already been stressed earlier, but it may do no harm to repeat how much a very few trained conservators and librarians technically competent to provide sensible orders and instruction could do to transform the relatively hidebound state of preservation. No skill is infinite, and its extension, in quantity and quality, is a low-cost option which holds the final key to the preservation problem on a national scale.

It is time for me to end and, searching for some means of coordinating these very disparate options, some universal key to the overall preservation problem, it seems to me that we have one here. I think that, in a sense, this gathering is itself the best augury for cooperative action in the future. Gone are the days when binding (and no distinction would be made between 'conservation' and 'binding') was a solitary craft, patronised but not publicised by its parent organisation. Academic staff, it may now be hoped, can see conservation as a task not to be relegated to the technicians, but as a combined operation, integral with the whole business of running a library, in which both sides have a duty to achieve mutual understanding and a mutually acceptable solution. Once our own house is in order, we can hope to extend the benefit of our experience to other countries, both in the Third World and elsewhere.

It would make a fine operatic conclusion to end there, on a cloud of grand strategy. But it is time to come back to earth with a bump. With the greatest exercise of economic planning, and greater goodwill, on all sides, present resources are inadequate for the basic needs, the foundation only, of a national preservation programme. We still cannot even, as the Canadians wish us to do, produce a national preservation policy. If a long and complicated past, plus a natural tendency to reticence, are a more serious obstacle than others may think, we cannot evade this duty indefinitely. Do we not know where to start? Is it so hard? Preservation, like charity, begins at home. A plan, any plan, is better than no plan. Public funds, however much needed, will not be made available for a national plan until individual libraries have put their own houses in order and, wherever possible, formed local cooperation plans of the kind Mr Turner is going to describe. This conference is a first step, an important step, towards a national preservation plan, and it will be seen as such. But if aspirations are to become reality, it will only come about if each and every library takes a realistic look at its stock and clientele, makes its own plan and begins to implement it.

Education and training for conservation work in the UK – B C Bloomfield, India Office Library and Records, British Library

1. The aim of this paper is briefly to set out the present state of education and training for conservation work and to try to indicate where there are gaps. The emphasis is on the needs of libraries and archives.

A. *Preamble*

2. Conservation work has most of the characteristics of an under-developed trade or profession, e.g.

    1. a small body of 'received' and agreed methods and practices (there is considerable dissent between practitioners as to 'good' and 'bad' methods);
    2. a fragmented, inadequate provision and dissemination of knowledge;
    3. no generally recognised job or career structure, educational standards for entry, or recognition of formal qualifications; and
    4. very few actual conservation posts established in major libraries and archives.

The Times (19 September 1983, p 29) in an article entitled 'Plenty of scope for Conservation' by John McCormick attempted to give a guide to the alleged multitude of job possibilities; the article does not mention paper, book or manuscript conservation at all. The Craft Council earlier in 1983 effctively withdrew its programme of grants to conservators to assist their training. There will be no replacement programme. The report of the Curriculum Development Project, *Curriculum change for the nineties*, by Edward Dudley, Eric Clough and E T Bryant (London, British Library, 1983) makes recommendations for re-shaping the training of professional librarians in the next 20 years; conservation and preservation get a passing mention in recommendation 25 (p 59). These three manifestations indicate that the biggest task is one of general education: to get librarians and others to recognise that a preservation problem exists. We need to heighten interest in preservation, bring it to the forefront of discussions, educate the general public and library authorities.

3. Training is a more definable problem, and libraries need training at various levels:

    1) *The research/consultancy level.* There already exist research projects funded by the British Library, research projects

undertaken and funded by the paper trades (Bowater, IPC, MacMillan Bloedel, etc), research by PIRA available on subscription or 'rental', research undertaken by the British Museum Laboratory, UMIST and other university and polytechnic research departments, but these projects' staff are not in touch with each other, nor are the results digested, tested and assessed for the bench practitioner. Existing abstracts services are slow in appearing and not widely diffused. The services of a testing or validating advisory service are also wanting.

2) *Librarians.* There is a need to educate practising librarians to be aware that the preservation problem exists and how problems can be met or rectified. This may primarily be a matter for professional associations, library schools, the professional press and private missionary work among practising librarians and line managers who take decisions on library materials.

3) *Librarians in training* need to be educated in conservation matters and problems as a necessary part of their training courses.

4) *Conservation workers* need training to carry out the actual tasks at the bench – including book binders.

5) *The general public, booksellers and publishers* need to be trained to be aware of conservation needs and problems so that they do not create problems for librarians unnecessarily.

6) *Overseas students* need training in our libraries, archives and facilities because they have no appropriate institutions in their own countries and look to the UK for help and advice. (Such help can be self-financing.)

4. What resources have we available to fill these needs? For the first our resources are probably adequate but not properly utilised or developed to communicate the results of research. For the second our resources are very poor. For the third, the report cited above, an article by Dr B S Benedikz (The guardianship of books: what must we know, in *Rare Books Group Newsletter*, 15 (May 1980), pp 5-15) and Mr Feather's contribution indicate that resources are insufficient. For the fourth there are courses at the Institute of Archaeology (University of London), Camberwell School of Art and Crafts, Gateshead and Colchester with lower level courses in other technical and further education colleges, plus the Society of Archivists scheme. For the fifth category nothing to my knowledge exists; and for the sixth category training attachments only are offered in the Public

Record Office and British Library (Bindery; India Office Library and Records; Department of Oriental Manuscripts and Printed Books).

5. It is imperative that library administrators should encourage professional associations for conservation such as the UK Institute for Conservation, the Institute for Paper Conservation, the annual instructional meeting for conservators organised by the Society of Archivists for many years (and open to librarians) and others. Proper professional standards in conservation work will ultimately be set by fully professional trained practitioners. To this must be allied improved and more speedy diffusion of research results to facilitate improvements in practice.

6. As corollaries there also need to be:

   i) improved manpower planning and forecasting in the conservation field in libraries and archives (LISC may help here);

   ii) the creation by library administrators (and others) of posts in conservation within library establishments to carry out the tasks identified as necessary;

   iii) the creation by library administrators (and others) of adequate career structures and progressive salary scales for conservation workers reflecting their status and importance; and

   iv) librarians and conservators must seek adequate (and higher) educational pre-entry qualifications for conservation trainees.

   This will also entail an examination of the old craft/trade apprenticeship training system to see if it might be re-structured to meet the conservation needs of large academic libraries and archives. It may also entail discussion and agreement with the appropriate trades unions.

B. *Existing training*

7. *Note* It is often difficult to discover what courses exist and syllabi are rapidly changing. The following list cannot be complete and I apologise for any inaccuracies it may contain. The Crafts Council issue a supplementary information sheet 'Training for conservation' which is revised periodically. Existing training courses have been roughly divided into three categories: full-time, part-time and 'on-the job'.

Full-time

Brunel Technical College, Ashley Down, Bristol BS7 9BU
Tel: Bristol (0272) 41241 ext 66.
Certificate in Bookbinding, Book Repair and Restoration together with paper and document conservation. 2 years. 4 GCE 'O'. Written practical and scientific work. City and Guilds Certificate, plus College Advanced Diploma.

Camberwell School of Art and Crafts, Peckham Road, London SE5 8UF
Tel: (01) 703-0987.
Diploma Course in Paper Conservation. 2 years. 3 GCE 'O'. Written, practical and scientific work. DATEC Diploma; leading on to –
Higher Diploma in Paper Conservation. 2 years. Preferably previous award of Diploma; otherwise unstated. Written, practical and scientific, plus administrative.
Optional specialisation in library, archival or illustrative materials. DATEC Higher Diploma. The college provides other courses for allied interests.

Colchester Institute, Sheepen Road, Colchester, Essex CO3 3LL
Tel: Colchester (0206) 70271.
Institute Diploma in Book Conservation. 2 years. 4 GCE 'O' and 1 GCE 'A'. (NB Suspended owing to financial cuts.)

Gateshead Technical College, Durham Road, Gateshead NE9 5BN
Tel: Gateshead (0632) 770524.
College Diploma in Conservation of Paintings. 2 years. 2 GCE 'A'. Mainly fine art, but includes general conservation documentation, prints and drawings, and paper.

Guildford County College of Technology, Stoke Park, Guildford, Surrey GU1 1EZ
Tel: Guildford (0483) 31251.
Diploma in Fine Bookbinding and Restoration. 2 years. 5 GCE 'O'. Theory practical work, design, etc. College diploma.

Lincoln College of Art, Lindum Road, Lincoln LN2 1NP
Tel: Lincoln (0522) 23267/9/0.
Diploma in Conservation Crafts. 2 years. 3 or 5 GCE 'O'. Scientific theory, art and design, craft skills. College diploma.

London College of Printing, Elephant and Castle, London SE1 6SB
Tel: (01) 735-8484; (01) 735-9100.
Craft Bookbinding. 1 year. Not given. College certificate. (NB. Other

courses offered full-time by the college do not appear to include hand processes.)

University of London Institute of Archaeology, 31-34 Gordon Square, London WC1H 0PY
Tel: (01) 387-6052.
BSc Archaeological Conservation. 3 years. 3 GCE 'A', including Chemistry. Mainly dealing with objects, but generally scientific and practical training.
MSc and PhD registrations for advanced work.
Institute Diploma in Conservation. Up to 4 years. Day release/part-time. Theoretical work, plus two years practical work and dissertation.
Special course for overseas students, Certificate in Conservation. 1 year.
(NB Three year courses leading to the Diploma in the Conservation of Paintings and the Diploma in the Conservation of Textiles [in cooperation with the Textile Conservation Centre, Hampton Court] are offered to graduates at the Courtauld Institute of Art in the University of London, 20 Portman Square, London W1H 0BE, Tel: (01) 935-9292/5.)

Part-time

Brighton Polytechnic, Moulsecoomb, Brighton BN2 4GJ
Tel: Brighton (0273) 67304/9.
Certificate in Bookbinding, Repair and Conservation. Minimum 3 years, maximum 6 years. None specified. Theory, practical, design, etc. Non-vocational. Part-time and evening.

Camberwell School of Art and Crafts, Peckham Road, London SE5
Tel: (01) 703-0987.
Practical Bookbinding. Not given. None specified. Evening.

Colchester Institute, Sheepen Road, Colchester, Essex CO3 3LL
Tel: Colchester (0206) 70271.
Certificate in Book Repair. 1 year. Not given. Part-time or evening.

Guildford County College of Technology, Stoke Park, Guildford, Surrey GU1 1EZ
Tel: Guildford (0483) 31251.
Fine Bookbinding and Restoration Course. 4 years. City & Guilds certificate or 5 GCE 'O', College certificate. Part-time.

London College of Printing, Elephant and Castle, London SE1 6SB
Tel: (01) 735-8484; (01) 735-9100.
Conservation of Library Material. 1 year. Not given. Evening. *Craft Bookbinding.* 1 year. Not given. Part-time. *Paper and Book Restoration.* 1 year. Part-time and evening. Not given.

Notes: The Society of Archivists believe that conservation courses are offered at a college in Portsmouth but I have been unable to trace details. The leaflet issued by the Crafts Advisory Council in 1979 also lists crafts bookbinding courses at Oxford Polytechnic, Reigate School of Art, Southampton College of Art, Twickenham College of Technology, Wolverhampton Polytechnic, Morley College and a number of adult education institutes in the GLC area.

'On the job'

a. Some of the colleges and institutes listed above offer sandwich or day-release classes for those in full-time employment seeking training and some are offered as part of courses leading to City and Guilds Institute of London qualifications or those sponsored by the Business Education Council (BEC). However since there are few established posts for conservators such courses are usually part of printing or bookbinding apprenticeships offered by trade houses. For bookbinding, it is worth noting that most trade apprentices are no longer taught the elements of craft bookbinding.

b. A number of pupils are taken by the elite bookbinder/designers such as Roger Powerll and Sandy Cockerell (among others), but these are few in number.

c. Book binderies established in academic and university libraries also produce some trained apprentices but, again these are few in number.

d. The laboratories and workshops established by the Public Record Office, British Library, British Museum and India Office Library and Records also take a few students each year for 'on-the-job' training. In certain cases students from overseas are accepted.

e. The Society of Archivists Training Scheme for archive conservationists. Established 1968 and operating from 1973. 24 weeks over 2 years. Part-time. Those in appropriate employment. Society's certificates. This scheme, entirely organised and run by the Society of Archivists, had trained 28 members employed in conservation work in local record offices in 1978.

C. *Gaps in training*

8. It is clear that there is little organised study of conservation methods or techniques at university level, although investigations are often undertaken or commissioned to solve particular conservation problems. London appears to be the only university offering such courses at the Institute of Archaeology. Camberwell School of Art and Crafts is the only college offering courses particularly designed for the needs of libraries and archives and involving three years full-time study. Output from both institutions is small.

9. It is unfortunately true that no library school in this country offers students training in conservation methods or management. There is no course which will acquaint librarians, senior or junior, with the elements of conservation methods and give an insight into technical and management problems.

10. If all major libraries and archives in the UK had established posts for conservators it seems likely that the present output of the courses available would be inadequate to fill those posts. (It may be that courses should be amalgamated and upgraded both as to content of syllabus and entry qualifications.)

11. In my view there are two major immediate gaps in coverage for conservation training:

    a. an intensive course of about three months designed to introduce practising experienced librarians to the problems, methods and materials of conservation and its management; and

    b. an intensive course of about three months designed to instil in junior librarians and technicians an elementary knowledge of the basic principles of conservation together with a number of basic practical skills.

    Both gaps might be filled by one course and it should be noted that there is considerable demand from librarians and archivists from overseas for such a course. (See annex.)

ANNEX

Conservation short courses: suggested aims and content

The aims of a course designed to fill these gaps might be to:

1. instil general theoretical knowledge of conservation and its principles as applied to library and archival materials;
2. give an introduction to, and some practice in, techniques of conservation – with some field work.

Method of study:

> Full-time attendance at a specified centre.

Length of course:

> Three months made up roughly of:
> 1. 1 month theory
> 2. 1 month laboratory work
> 3. 2 weeks practical field work in a designated library or archive
> 4. 1 week examination
> 5. 1 week administration

Sponsors of the course:

British Library, Public Record Office, British Council, Society of Archivists.

Host for the course:

A technical college (or possibly the BL, PRO or Bodleian). The great majority of students will be in or near London, and also in the largest libraries and archives.

Frequency of the course:

> Once or twice each calendar year.

Number of student places:

12

Type of students to be trained:

> Probably mainly in two categories: professional librarians and archivists

wanting to become familiar with conservation methods, and junior staff from smaller institutions wanting speedy, elementary training in a range of conservation techniques and not willing to enrol for the two-year course. (There may be a conflict here in basic educational background which will render it expedient to set a minimum educational level for entry.) In addition there will be students from the book industries (publishing, binding, etc.) and from the antiquarian book trade. There will be a considerable demand from overseas students, mainly sponsored by their libraries and archives. It will certainly be necessary to see that these candidates are not unsuitable low-level staff. Defined in reverse, the course will be for all those unwilling to study for two years and become full-blown conservators.

It will be necessary to try to forecast the demand for places from libraries and archives in the UK. (IOLR has taken the following numbers of trainees in the last few years: 1974 – 14; 1975 – 12; 1976 – 7; 1977 – 11; 1978 – 10; 1979 – 4 (estimate). Each year it has turned away four or five candidates.)

Cost:

If such a course is established it will need priming finance. The host will need to plan and estimate recurrent costs and these should be completely recovered from fees. There may need to be expenditure on equipment which should not fall on the host.

I am indebted for help in writing this paper to Mr Sears, Information Officer of the City and Guilds Institute of London, but he is in no way responsible for the opinions expressed.

Conservation education for professional librarians: a library school view - J Feather, Department of Library and Information Studies, Loughborough University

Chapter 6 of the report of the British Library Conservation Project makes melancholy reading for those concerned with conservation in our libraries. Although some training facilities seem to exist for benchworkers and technicians, it is clear that the study of conservation is almost entirely lacking from professional library education. In the next few pages I would like to suggest some ways in which we can remedy this situation, bearing in mind the financial and physical constraints under which the schools must necessarily operate for the foreseeable future. The comparative scarcity of educational resources, and the very real prospect of their further diminution, means that if we are to justify major new developments, such as this would be, such developments must be carefully matched to the needs of the profession.

In considering this matter, we have to start from first principles, for it seems that little thought has previously been given to the matter. For example, the recently published British Library report, *Curriculum change for the nineties* has nothing to say on the subject of conservation. We should, I think, distinguish between two separate, although related, aspects of the topic. First, there is the need which is repeatedly, and properly, emphasised throughout the Conservation Project report for a greater awareness of the importance of the subject among librarians, and for some understanding of its ramifications and implications. Secondly, there is a need for a greater dissemination of the technical skills which are needed for the actual repair and preservation of materials. I shall say very little about the latter, although it is, of course, of the utmost importance, and I am assured by conservators that there is a great shortage of people with appropriate technical expertise and scientific knowledge. Technical education of this kind, however, important as it is, is not a matter for the library schools. Increasing awareness and understanding, on the other hand, is very much a matter for library educators, and I would like to consider some of the ways in which this can be done.

There are several levels on which conservation could be introduced into library school syllabuses. We could simply strengthen its existing representation, which is largely confined to courses on rare books, archives, special collections, and the like; we could find some way of incorporating it more generally into the core courses; or we could, as some schools have, I understand, already suggested consider the possibility of full-scale courses in the subject leading, perhaps, to a Master's degree. All of these notions have something to commend them, and they are not mutually exclusive. To choose between them, or to establish an order of priorities for their introduction, we must, however, attempt to define a little more closely exactly what it is that we would be trying to do.

The conservation crisis which confronts our libraries wil not only persist, it will probably become worse. In other words, if we are to cope logically and intelligently with the situation in which we find ourselves, we need to plan for the future. The careful and highly skilled repair of a few manuscripts and early printed books, however individually important they may be, does not solve the larger problem of the rapid deterioration, and in extreme cases virtual disintegration, of library stocks. This is a problem for all libraries, even those which envisage a comparatively short lifespan for large parts of their stock. The need is to extend that life to whatever length is thought appropriate, whether it is five years or indefinitely, and whether the material concerned is a medieval manuscript or a floppy disk. Put in this way, it is, I hope, clear that conservation is at least as much a problem of management as it is of scientific, technical and artistic skill. It is also a general problem in libraries of all kinds and all sizes, and is not confined to the great research libraries with their commitment to the long-term preservation of materials.

From this, it follows that there is a strong case for the incorporation of conservation in some form into the core courses of all professional library education. It also, I think, follows, that the appropriate areas of the core in which the subject should be incorporated is that of management. This is not merely an administrative convenience; I believe that, in the light of what I have just said, this would be the most logical approach. Conservation in its broadest sense might, indeed, properly be described as collection management, a process which begins not when a book starts to show visible signs of deterioration, but when it first enters the library. Just as all libraries have policies, whether written or not, which largely determine their book selection, so there is a need for similar policies to determine what categories of material it is intended to preserve and for how long. It follows that the environment in which different parts of the stock are housed will, ideally, be appropriate to their intended life. All of these matters are clearly aspects of management, and it is in that context that they should be introduced into library school syllabuses as a matter of urgency.

It has to be admitted, however, that in-depth study will not be possible because of the time constraints, especially in the crucial one-year postgraduate courses which will produce the bulk of future generations of senior librarians. Nevertheless, even a few hours devoted to such matters in the same course in which personnel and financial management are discussed will not only emphasise the importance which we attach to them, but will also place them in the proper context. The collection is the library's largest and only permanent resource, and needs to be handled with the same care and professional skill which is applied to handling, for example, the budget.

To be credible and useful, however, such a course will have to teach students something beyond mere generalisations about the conservation of materials. It is neither possible nor desirable to avoid some teaching of the scientific basis of conservation, even if it will, necessarily, be in very general terms of the physical nature of library materials and their preferred environments. Even that little, I would emphasise, is better than is normally achieved at present. Despite the constraints of time, and the conflicting demands of other subjects, it ought to be possible to ensure that no-one enters the profession without an understanding of the problem in general terms, and enough specific knowledge to be able to take decisions about binding, storage, and so on, which will achieve whatever conservation objectives a particular library may have set itself.

All of this obviously has resource implications for the schools themselves, but before dealing with that, I should like to say a little about the possibility of more specialised and detailed conservation courses. Traditionally, such cursory treatment as conservation has received has been, as I said earlier, in the context of rare books and manuscripts. Those schools which continue to offer such courses, and contrary to the popular impression there are some which are totally committed to doing so, must recognise that conservation ought to be given greater prominence. I say this in the knowledge that I am as guilty as the next man of neglecting it. The archivist or the rare book librarian has to take conservation decisions whose effects may be felt for centuries to come, and some such set of guidelines as Nicholas Pickwoad has suggested should always be at their side. In other words, for those students who choose to specialise in rare books or archives, there is a need for study in greater depth than will be possible in the core course for the majority. Of course, the mere presence of conservation and collection management in the core will to some extent ease the problem in specialised courses, which at present must start from first principles, but which could certainly pursue conservation in more detail if it could be assumed that all students already had some basic knowledge of the subject.

I now come to the third of the possible lines of development, that of specialised courses. These could take the form either of full degree courses or of options within existing courses. Of the two, the latter seems far preferable, whatever the superficial attractions of the former. The role of the library schools in conservation education is, as I suggested at the beginning, to educate professional librarians in conservation awareness at various levels of expertise; it is not the object of the exercise to produce conservators, a very necessary task, but one better undertaken elsewhere. The report mentions the Master's programme in conservation at Columbia, but I do not believe that a comparable course would be appropriate in the UK. Quite apart from the fact that the job market in the US is very much larger than our own, it is, at least as far as conservation goes, in one significant respect very different. The great independent research libraries of North America have, in general, far greater flexibility in the allocation of their resources than have the publicly funded research libraries of the UK. Therefore, those American research libraries which wish to assign a high priority to conservation, as many of the more enlightened are now doing, can, in many cases, redirect funding from other areas into the conservation field. The possibility of anything similar happening in the UK, certainly to the point at which highly specialised staff are required, is very remote. In short, it is very difficult to see what demand there would be in the UK for the graduates of a postgraduate course in conservation. It may indeed be the case that such courses would have the potential for attracting overseas students, especially those from developing countries, but I shall return to that in a moment.

That leaves us with the possibility of a specialised option within the existing generic courses, in addition to giving conservation a place in the core and in appropriate existing options. This is something which ought to be pursued, for there would, I think, be a role for a professional librarian with a conventional qualification and some special expertise in conservation.

Finally, I should like to consider briefly the resource implications for the library school themselves. Because we have no tradition of teaching conservation, it follows that we do not have qualified staff to teach it. To undertake a complete programme of the kind I have suggested, there would be a need for at least a half-time lecturer with expertise in the field. On the other hand, the introduction of conservation into the core, which is the most immediately urgent problem, could be done by existing staff if they sought the assistance of outside experts. For more specialised courses, greater expertise would obviously be needed and would have to have some scientific and benchwork skills. Hence facilities would be needed for the demonstration of techniques, even though training in such techniques would be inappropriate. Clearly, such developments need to be funded. Although the sums of money involved would be comparatively modest, it is probable that at least a part of the initial costs would have to be sought from external sources. Once established, I have no doubt that the expertise and facilities could generate an income for the school and its parent institution through short courses of the kind envisaged by Barry Bloomfield in his paper annexed to the report. Such courses would attract both UK librarians and those from overseas, for there is a need for practising professionals, at every level, to develop their understanding of this field.

It cannot be said too often that we have reached crisis point in the preservation of the contents of our libraries, both great and small. If we are to resolve that crisis satisfactorily, we can only do so by an effort of political will to redirect resources according to our judgment of priorities. This applies as much in the field of education and training as it does in the libraries themselves. I hope that I have suggested to you some of the ways in which we could incorporate this important subject into the existing pattern of British library education. My suggestions have been deliberately modest in scope, but I nevertheless believe that we must make an immediate start in their implementation if we are to ensure that our successors will have a chance of solving some of the problems with which we are now confronted.

Conservation binding – Nicholas Pickwood, Conservator and Institute of Paper Preservation, Norwich

At a recent seminar, a librarian announced that he left all his conservation problems to his binder and that he did not discuss with the binder the treatment which each volume was to get. The statement revealed a dangerous confusion about the nature of conservation work, as well as an extraordinarily cavalier attitude on the part of the librarian. Conservation is not simply a smart word for binding, but a complex discipline, involving actual repair work, though not necessarily binding. It demands not only a high level of craft skill, but also an acute historical and aesthetic awareness and knowledge, a familiarity with library practice, shelving and use (for books cannot be repaired without a knowledge of their storage and use) and a proper awareness of the chemistry of sound materials and deterioration. Beyond this, there is a need for an effective exchange of information between the conservator and the library staff, for all are concerned in preserving the library's *raison d'être* – its books. Conservation and preservation policies will be stunted if they are served only by technicians chained to a bench. Conservation expertise must be involved in decisions which involve the physical well-being of the books, for it is too late when the conservators are asked to put right the damage caused by badly designed buildings and shelving or by bad exhibition conditions. Good conservators are trained to know and care about these things, and have valuable help to offer.

Not all binders are conservation binders; in fact, there are very few binders who can claim to carry out proper conservation work, and understanding the differences between the different types of binder is a vital prerequisite to being able to embark on an effective conservation programme. To understand why there are different types of binder, it is necessary to take a brief historical excursion, and it should help to clear up a terminological confusion which has grown up around the terms 'trade' and 'craft'. These terms are often used very inexactly, and frequently with pejorative overtones (which work both ways) that make it difficult for the non-expert to assess the relevance and value of the different types of work offered to him.

The distinction begins to appear with the invention of printing. When all books were written by hand, the binder, who worked right through the binding process and thus had a grasp of the 'whole' book, was able to treat the individual book with individual care, selecting materials and structures to suit its need with great craft sophistication. In doing so, he was able to create effective long lasting books which did no damage to the leaves as an integral part of the binding process. They were, in effect, true conservation bindings, and fine finish was not a prime consideration.

The spread of printing in the 16th century meant that binders were exposed to two new influences. First, there was a vastly greater output of material requiring binding, and secondly, for the first time there were indentical text-blocks being bound, which made it possible and commercially desirable to begin the business of standardisation. As a result, structural standards began to fall as the binders began to cut corners. Many of the short cuts which are associated with the 19th century, such as stuck on endbands, were in fact well established by the end of the 16th century. In the 17th century, it was not uncommon for binders to use false raised bands and even glued bindings on books which were deliberately made to look as if they were better constructed. At an early date, therefore, inferior structural work was being made to look like something better, and the appearance of quality became an important consideration. Whilst materials of reasonable quality were still the norm, comparatively durable structures were still produced, as is evident from the thousands of 18th century and earlier bindings which still survive. However, when technological advances made it possible to manufacture poor quality materials on a large scale, this safeguard no longer applied, and continuing pressures to speed up production and keep prices down led to still further reductions in the quality of binding structures. Appearance began to dominate, and only by skimping on materials and structures could the trade binderies, in hot economc competition, keep their prices down. Anyone familiar with the slick finish and detached boards of so many late 19th century bindings will know what this resulted in. Our problem today is that much of what is called fine binding is inherited from these essentially debased techniques. With the apparent acquiescence of their clients, which included the libraries, the binders had no incentive to raise their standards. Expert in doing their job, these big trade binderies had devoted their considerable expertise into forcing the old binding skills into patterns dictated by cost and not function. Low costs were maintained by running the workshops on a production line basis, so that one workman no longer made the whole book, and the practice of binding was increasingly laid down according to rules which may have been economically sensible, but which were founded in no strict craft logic. Consequently, as the variety of structures available to the binder was increasingly eliminated, so the average binder's ability to grasp the full possibilities of structure become atrophied. This was to have serious consequences for the repair of early books, where the now conventional trade skills were applied to structures lying well outside the scope of those skills. When this narrowing of techniques is combined with a virtual collapse in the quality of materials, one is left with a tradition of binding whose only relevance to conservation is to create a need for it.

It was in reaction to the deteriorating quality of fine binding that the first craft revival binders, led by Cobden-Sanderson, took a fresh and in many ways a backward look at binding, learning from the past how to make durable new structures. The most influential exponent of this revival was Douglas Cockerell, whose book, *Bookbinding and the care of books*, of 1901 remains one of the most useful books on the subject. However, Cockerell's attempts at the W H Smith bindery to bring these revived skills into the trade met with limited success, and the craft tradition became established as something distinct from the trade. It is worth noting that Cockerell was regarded with distrust by the tutors from the trade who taught with him at the Central School in the 1930s.

This division was particularly sad, because it was from the craft tradition that the special disciplines of book conservation emerged, started by Douglas Cockerell, and developed by Sidney Cockerell and Roger Powell. It was from this tradition that the major contribution came to the rescue operation after the Florence floods in 1966, and subsequently, most of the significant developments in conservation have come from the same source. The important workshops at the Library of Congress, Trinity College Dublin, Bodley and the University of Texas have all been built up by craft binders, and the 1980 Cambridge Conference also came out of the same stable. As a reminder that the craft tradition is not simply interested in small numbers of fine bindings, it should be noted that from these workshops emerged such major conservation developments as phase boxing, heat-set tissues and polyester encapsulation. In very much simplified terms, the repair of books in this discipline becomes a question of technical, historical and aesthetic standards selected to suit the individual book, its structure, condition and future use. It should not involve obliging the book to fit into a straightjacket of narrowly based trade techniques. Whether the book in question is a major treasure or one of a run of periodicals, if the books are intended for permanent retention, the same criteria must apply, for it is essential that the quality of the work required is accurately assessed and is best suited to the job in hand. There is simply no point in repair if it destroys the very qualities that you want to preserve, and there is no point in binding, rebinding or repairing any book intended for permanent retention if it is going to fall apart after a few years.

It is at this point that quality becomes a matter of overriding importance. Without sustained high quality in materials, workmanship and also in the decision-making which should initiate conservation work, the conservation of books is a waste of time, effort and money. It also has to be recognised that in all conservation work, the achievement and maintenance of high quality has to be the main criterion, and not output. When the high quality has been achieved and steps taken to maintain it, ways of increasing output can be considered. If work of poor quality is produced, the problems to be faced are simply multiplied wholesale, and, in fact, the faster you manage to bind or repair the books, the worse the problem will become. In many libraries this is now happening, and the work is simply piling up impossible problems for our successors.

The first essential in achieving the right quality is to procure and then use *only* materials of adequate quality. If binders cannot get such material, the expenditure in time and money on conservation will be wasted. Anyone with eyes can see the quality of materials used on early books, but materials of this quality are simply not available today. Every month, it seems, another firm goes out of business, taking with it vital materials (the only durable calfskin was recently lost this way). Modern hand-made paper has little of the strength of early papers. Constantly, specifications are changed without reference to the conservators who are using the relevant materials, but the materials are passed off as being the same quality, and perhaps unknowingly the conservator will waste his time and his employer's money by using it. Ranges of materials are reduced, limiting the ability of the binder to suit structures to weight and function. Expertise disappears so that detailed specifications cannot be drawn up. If we acquiesce in this situation and simply accept what we are given, we will not be thanked by our successors. The report indicates that only 19 libraries are worried about the quality of materials. This means that those of the remaining 313 libraries which wish to retain any books permanently are either fools or worse. It is vital that all these libraries cooperate and give their support to attempts to secure the right materials and encourage firms to supply what is needed.

As well as materials, the quality of the design and execution of conservation work is of crucial importance, and this applies equally to mass binding as well as one-off work. If a book does not work properly, it will be forced in use and broken, and a technique such as cleat sewing, which almost inevitably results in a very limited ability to open, is thus highly unsuitable for permanent work. It also makes books extremely difficult and expensive to repair or rebind in the future, and it cannot therefore be counted as a conservation technique. The whole question of the design of suitable bindings for this category of work needs to be looked at very carefully to ensure that the best use is being made of the effort at present being put into it. There are better answers, and this is an area where the 'trade' and the 'craft' need to work together.

For the repair of rare books, there are no blanket answers, and little or no scope for production line techniques. Instead, there is an immense range of treatments which can be used to prolong the useful life of the books we wish to preserve intact. In place of the once near obligatory rebinding (an attitude still being taught), there are now available techniques for repairing and supporting weak structures without destroying the original and without the heavy reliance on glue that is causing such immense and expensive problems when further repair becomes necessary.

The report mentions boxing as an alternative to repair and an ideal way of securing books without the loss of historic structures, indications of provenance and character. Some libraries have had sophisticated boxing programmes for some years now, but few other libraries have followed suit. Yet there is no better, safer or cheaper method of preserving fragile, damaged and vulnerable material. Boxes may range from the individually tailored drop-back box intended for permanent use to the cheap and rapidly made phase boxes, which can stabilise a desperate situation and buy time in which to work out permanent preservation measures. By such means, the repair work which has destroyed so much of the historical character of our books – and which libraries have an obligation to preserve – can be avoided.

If a book is to be repaired, then it must work – that is, withstand use and protect the contents. Failure to achieve these ends is graphically illustrated by the repair of vellum leaved manuscripts. Vellum is not paper and it reacts differently and violently to the moisture in glue when it is applied to it. Thus, when the spines of such books are glued up, the vellum cockles and the spine becomes completely inflexible. The damage done to these books in financial terms over the past 200 years is frightening, quite apart from the historical and physical damage. Yet it is still happening. Earlier this year, a Cambridge College Library sent out manuscripts with the instruction that no more than £35 was to be spent on any one book. For each £35 thus spent (and the sum is scarcely adequate to afford even a proper examination of a single manuscript), the college may well find themselves paying hundreds of pounds or more at some future date in undoing the damage caused by the cheap repairs. It is a straightforward matter to bind these books so that they work properly, but it makes reference to scarcely a single technique to be found in the training of the average trade binder.

This sort of treatment is becoming increasingly common, as interest in conservation outgrows any awareness of what is involved in the work. In addition, there are firms of binders, deprived of traditional work, who, simply by calling themselves conservators, hope to jump onto the new bandwagon without any qualifications. That they are able to do so is a comment on the ability of the people who are using them. When such binders repair books with structures they do not understand, such as limp vellum bindings, the results, instead of being safe and convenient to handle, are all too often impossible to open and unsafe to read without damaging the book. When such structures are explained to the students on a leading conservation course, and they ask 'are you allowed to do that?', then it is evident that there is something seriously wrong with their training.

When things go wrong, it is frequently because of a failure by both binder and client, and is the result of an insensitivity to the materials involved and, more often, a startling lack of imagination. It is one thing not to have enough money to do a job properly, but another to do it on the cheap and thus make inevitable the need for massive expense to undo the damage thus caused. It must also be remembered that much of the damage caused by such work can never be undone. The principle of reversible repairs is slowly becoming established, but less well recognised is that the fact that repairs which have been carried out cannot be reversed. In treating books hitherto untouched by repairs, there is only one chance to make the right decisions. Historical evidence cannot be recreated.

These things happen because of a lack of proper training, or, in other words, ignorance. This applies not only to work on the bench, but also to where the decisions are being made about conservation work. These decisions can only be made on the basis of knowledge, and crash courses for librarians are not going to give them the in-depth knowledge that is required. But at the same time, how many binders are aware, or are even encouraged to become aware, of the significance of what they are asked to handle? The result in our rare book collections is continuing historical destruction. One would hope that it would be impossible for a copy of the first edition of Donne's poems in contemporary calf to be rebound now in gold tooled morocco 'so as better to suit the importance of the book'. But this happened within the last four years in one of our cathedral libraries. It should seem incredible that our few remaining Romanesque bindings, with all that they may have to tell us about the manuscripts they protect, might still be destroyed by rebinding, but such work is still being carried out.

One is forced to ask why these shoddy, inadequate and damaging repairs are still carried out. A lack of money is not a sufficient excuse. A lack of knowledge would appear to be the main culprit. There are certainly many binders who are incapable of the tasks set them, but who sets the tasks and chooses the binder? How many people who have the task of ordering repairs are sufficiently informed, historically and technically, to specify work of the right quality? The ultimate responsibility lies with the librarians, and it should be they who set the standards. But to do this, they will need the expertise of trained conservators as well as their own, and to obtain this expertise, we will need not only more money, but quite simply the establishment of a proper training course for conservators, for there is none in existence at present, and some training in conservation awareness for librarians. Without a commitment to expand our scarce resources, financial and human, and a continuing commitment to use them effectively and carefully to the lasting benefit of our library heritage, we will be falling down on a major commitment to future generations, and bequeathing to them not books, but problems.

Training conservation technicians: an archivist's view - D Thomas, Public Record Office, London

My intention is to consider the proposals of this report which relate to the training of technicians and to provide an outsider's view of these ideas. I have been involved in the training of conservation technicians at the Public Record Office and as an assessor on the Society of Archivists' training scheme, and also have evaluated one of the courses run by a college on behalf of the Technician Education Council.

This report proposes that librarians should seek to promote binding and conservation training in appropriate educational institutions; existing provisions should be expanded and rationalized. At the same time, the problems of pay and conditions of service for technicians should be reviewed at a national level to remedy the situation in which it is more lucrative for binders to undertake low-skilled high production work or to become self employed craftsmen than it is for them to accept employment in libraries.

Before discussing these ideas, I ought to say something about conservation in record offices. As the report makes clear, archivists are more concerned with this matter than are librarians. All qualified archivists have some training in this area and most institutions have conservation facilities in-house; a few smaller ones rely on the services of other offices or use private conservators.

Technicians come from four major sources. Some are former print trade binders who have moved into this related field, but such staff do require further training before they are competent conservators. Others come from the sort of training courses described in Mr Bloomfield's paper, but most employers find that they do require further training before they can be given a high level of responsibility. A number have been trained at the major national institutions such as the Public Record Office, but such sources are less productive than they once were.

The most important source is the in-service training scheme run by the Society of Archivists. This was established in 1973 to meet precisely the sort of need for trained craftsmen described in the present report. It is essentially a cooperative training venture. Trainees are employed in record offices and spend two years gaining experience of the work. Twenty-four weeks are spent in formal instruction in their own or other offices. During these periods of instruction, training is provided in a range of techniques and methods defined in a detailed syllabus. There is a week of lectures and visits. Assessment is by means of reports from the instructing offices, a written paper and an oral examination at which examples of the candidates' work are seen. Trainees range from school leavers to qualified binders.

Control over the scheme is exercised by the Society of Archivists through its technical and training committees, while immediate supervision is provided by a voluntary registrar and a committee consisting of the chairman of the assessment panel, the chairman of the technical committee and an archival conservator who has acted as an instructor.

So far, the venture has met the needs of the Society of Archivists; 52 candidates have been trained and received certificates of competence and possession of such a certificate is normally required of applicants for posts as conservators in record offices.

This scheme may prove a useful model for librarians. It is an example of a related profession controlling the training and influencing the standards of qualifications for conservators. There are dangers of leaving training in the hands of appropriate educational institutions. First, it may prove difficult to ensure that such colleges set appropriate standards. Secondly, and more importantly, it may be difficult to control the contents of their courses. Colleges tend to be influenced by the availability of particular skills amongst their staff and by the demands of students. There is a real risk that they could produce graduates whose abilities do not always match the precise needs of libraries. Do libraries, for example, really need a lot of staff trained in the conservation of prints and drawings?

It may not be necessary or practical for libraries to be directly involved in training conservators. It would, however, be beneficial for librarians as a profession to address themselves to the problem of deciding precisely what training conservators should be given and perhaps to work towards the establishment of a nationally recognised qualification for library conservators.

Once such a qualification were established, then it would prove easier to deal with the problems of the pay and conditions of service for technicians outlined in the report. Indeed, it may not prove possible to solve such problems without first setting up a nationally agreed standard for training.

I must express one slight personal disappointment in that the report says far too little about the problems of third world countries. If the problems of British libraries are bad, those in many third world countries are worse. If our training facilities are not perfect, those in many countries are non-existent. National institutions in the UK are showered with requests to train technicians from overseas. Can I express the hope that if any new training initiative does emerge as a result of this excellent report, it does contain some provision for training conservators from poorer countries.

Conservation in the Bodleian: a case study - M L Turner, The Bodleian Library, Oxford

The Conservation Section was set up in the Bodleian in September 1978. A new post - Head of Conservation - was created in the central administration under the Secretary of the Library, and Michael L Turner, previously Head of Special Collections within the Department of Printed Books, was appointed to this position. The section was created by bringing together several existing areas of responsibility within the Library, in order to help the Head of Conservation in carrying out his brief of taking care of the storage and physical condition of the books and manuscripts throughout the Bodleian system.

The largest element absorbed in the new section was the Bookstack and Book Service centred in the New Library building, under the superintendence of Mr Jack Webster. Mr Webster and his staff are not only responsible for the arrangement and care of 11 floors of closed bookstacks, but also for providing a book service to the many reading areas in the Old Library, the Radcliffe Camera and the New Library itself. Over the last few years this has meant dealing with an average of around a quarter of a million orders a year, not only fetching the requested items from the shelves but subsequently returning them to their correct places. In addition to the New Library bookstacks, responsibility was accepted for the storage of books at the University's Libraries Board repository outside Oxford at Nuneham Courtenay. The Conservation Section also acts in an advisory capacity regarding the storage of books in the Bodleian's dependent libraries housed in separate buildings - the Radcliffe Science Library, the Law Library and Rhodes House Library. The Indian Institute Library's books are housed in the New Library bookstacks.

Secondly, the Library Bindery under the supervision of Mr Ron Harvey and already within the Library's administrative service, became central to the new section's concern. At this time, Mr Harvey's bindery was performing all the necessary repair work for maintaining the main Library's open-shelf material, also providing such repair work as was being done on the older bindings in the Library's collections, including the making of protective boxes for special items. Beyond this Mr Harvey was responsible for the organisation of all the binding being sent out of the Library to external commercial binderies.

Thirdly, a small 'paper repair' workshop, under Mrs Judy Segal in the Department of Western Manuscripts came over into the new Conservation Section. This workshop had just been re-housed and to some extent re-equipped in the Clarendon Building. Mrs Segal was highly respected among paper conservators, and had been instrumental along with Dr David

Cooper in the development of the application of enzymes in the removal of certain types of old adhesive in conservation work.

From the beginning it was agreed that a further senior position should be created directly under the Head of Conservation – that of a Conservation Officer, with a high level of practical knowledge and skills. The Library was extremely fortunate in acquiring the services of Mr Christopher Clarkson, undoubtedly one of the best known book conservators in Europe and North America. Mr Clarkson, whose early training and experience was in the UK, came to the Library from the USA where he had held the position of Head of Conservation of Rare Books in the Library of Congress and several consultancy positions with major art galleries. For many years he was also very closely involved in the aftermath of the disastrous flood in Florence of December 1966. It was also possible to retain the services of Dr Cooper as a consultant on scientific matters.

There was no large initial grant of money to set up the Conservation Section. The only finance available was that which was already provided each year for the various areas already described. Up until this time the bulk of this money was spent on external binding, and it was clear that if progress was to be made in other directions there would have to be a switch in the way in which these limited resources were applied.

Several areas of concern emerged in the first year or so of the section's work. In the first place, it was apparent that the grade and salary levels of the binders and the conservators were not high enough within the existing structure of the Library to ensure that we would retain our qualified staff or attract the right kind of people in the future. After a long negotiation with the university this position has at least been improved.

Secondly, in a library that occupies buildings on several sites, which vary in date from the middle of the 15th century to the 1970s, environmental conditions are not an easy problem with which to deal. Controlling temperatures and relative humidity, and reconciling the different needs of staff and readers on the one hand with those of the Library's holdings on the other becomes an even more difficult operation under these circumstances. A great deal of extremely expensive structural work will have to be carried out in future years to make the necessary alterations and to install a suitable monitoring system in order to achieve a controlled environment in which to preserve our books and manuscripts. The Curators of the Library have just decided to commission a consultant to advise on this situation within the New Library bookstacks.

Thirdly, it was necessary to expand and equip the bindery and workshop facilities for the Conservation Section. Initially, it was hoped that the

Clarendon Building might prove a suitable place in which to do this, especially as the paper repair workshop had recently been installed in that building. After a certain amount of planning and work with the University Surveyor's department, this proved to be impracticable – again the age and historic importance of the building itself caused too many problems. It was decided, therefore, to alter some rooms on the second floor of the New Library, adjacent to the bookstack and therefore much more suitable for the purpose, into working areas for a specialist bindery, an additional flat paper conservation area, and a new and enlarged box making room, alongside the main office of the section. This is proceeding slowly – two of the three areas are now in use, and it is hoped that the specialist bindery will be operating in its new room very shortly. This is not to say that these areas are now fully equipped, but the basic layout of benches, sinks and the like will have been provided, and gradually over the next few years the necessary equipment will have to be found. Unfortunately, this has left Mrs Segal and her Conservation Workshop isolated in the Clarendon Building. Our long term plans must aim at re-uniting her with the rest of the section.

Gradually, the section will have to build up a condition report on much of the Library's holdings. This has begun. At weekly meetings the various departments and dependent libraries meet with the section to bring work forward, and, perhaps more importantly, to discuss longer term problems and areas of concern. In this way, and also by going into the stack to make specific reports, we are gradually building up a record on which to plan future work and base our arguments for the provision of future resources. In a library of the size of the Bodleian this is no small task, and the section is already considering using a microprocessor to control its records.

As there was little money and very little workshop space in which to carry out much work in the early stages, it was decided to concentrate initially on a system of protection for the Library's material. Practically all outside binding was stopped for the materials in the main bookstacks – a decision made easier by the rising costs and falling quality of such work. The money thus saved became our main resource for creating the new working areas, and for initiating a connected series of specially designed archival quality envelopes, folders and boxes, which are made for us by an outside firm. By using these, and further individually designed phase boxes and special boxes, we hope over the next few years to provide at least some protection for much of the Library's damaged, and more valuable material.

Of course, this programme in itself will not solve the problem, the material is still in need of attention and repair; but, as everything that received protection is also subjected to a conservation survey, we are gradually learning what the problems are and where our efforts must be directed.

Education is also one of the major tasks of any library conservation unit; educating readers, staff and those who control the purse strings – not only in the handling of material and in its storage, but also into a passionate belief that the idea of conservation has to enter into each and every aspect of the Library's business, and that a major part of the Library's resources must be devoted to it, if we are to stand any reasonable chance of handing on to future generations the incredible heritage and resources that we ourselves inherited and have been privileged to use.

In a worsening financial situation since 1978, the authorities in the Bodleian have grasped the problem and within the limits of their present resources are devoting an ever increasing slice of the cake to conservation, but the problems are enormous, and the funds needed will be immense. Consequently the theme of conservation is central to the Librarian's recent 'A development plan for the Bodleian Library, 1982-2002'. In his plan the Librarian has 'identified four areas of activity which inter-relate and which, taken together, offer the possibility of arresting and redressing the deterioration of the collections, and of improving control over them and of improving access to the Library's great resources'.

Under the general heading of 'Conservation' the Librarian speaks of the general problems in this area facing all major libraries, and concludes – 'More money is required, however, to recruit, train and employ staff, to equip workspaces, to provide materials and to facilitate the record-keeping associated with the work of the Section'.

Under the more specific heading 'The environment of the book-stack' the Librarian points out that money spent on conservation in the narrower sense 'may be wasted if the book is then returned to a storage environment which is inimical to the longevity of the materials'. He continues – 'There is a need for the design and implementation in the New Library stack of a new air-conditioning system to maintain an even environment, within as narrow limits of temperature and humidity as possible and ensure the cleaning and exchange of the air'.

The third area isolated in the Librarian's report, which specifically relates to the preservation of the Library's materials is 'Protective photography'. The plan is 'to substitute the consultation of a copy for that of the original' in large areas of the collections. 'The copy may be a published facsimile, a microfilm or microfiche, or, in the future, a video image stored on a magnetic medium such as disc or tape.... Here again, the requirement is principally for manpower, materials, equipment and workspace. The newer technology of video may also require some research into systems and techniques. The resulting copies then need strictly controlled environments for long-term storage without degradation.... We also need a record-keeping and cataloguing system to ensure that the copy, rather than the original, is offered to the reader as soon as it is available. As the number of copies grows, the difficulties of achieving a quickly modified catalogue increase'.

This final point leads into the fourth and final area of the development plan – 'Information technology' and demonstrates very clearly how a comprehensive conservation programme concerns all aspects of the library's planning for the future. To implement these far reaching proposals will clearly need a very large input of funds and consequently the primary aim of the Library must be to obtain these funds to allow for any progress to be made along the lines indicated.

Other reports

Library and Information Research (LIR) Reports may be purchased from Publications Section, British Library Lending Division, Boston Spa, Wetherby, West Yorkshire LS23 7BQ, UK. Details of some other LIR Reports are given below.

Computer software: supplying it and finding it by W Tagg and R Templeton
LIR Report 10   ISBN 0 7123 3014 3
Following the 1981 seminar on 'Libraries and computer materials', a representative survey of the various agencies involved in the production and distribution of computer software was carried out. The results of the survey are used: a) to give a broad indication of the state of publishing in this area; and b) to show the various data elements employed in the description and recording of information about software. An examination of the elements in b) provides the basis for some observations about cataloguing requirements, and for comparison with existing guidelines.

An investigation of the use of systems programs in library applications of microcomputers by A Trevelyan and M Rowat
LIR Report 12   ISBN 0 7123 3017 8
For various areas of library activity readily available software tools might be used as alternatives to the writing of dedicated applications programs for systems based on microcomputers. This report examines six areas in detail: circulation control, acquisitions, cataloguing, notification, small databases, and periodicals circulation. The approach adopted offers the basis of a fast and relatively cheap method of implementing systems for particular applications in libraries.

Libraries bring Prestel to the public: a summary of British Library-supported research 1979-1981 by Judy Redfearn
LIR Report 13   ISBN 0 7123 3019 4
Between 1979 and 1981 the British Library supported research into Prestel to see if it could assist in the two main roles of libraries: the dissemination of published information, and the publication of local information. Prestel sets were installed in different types of library throughout the country, and public libraries and local authorities were invited to become members of an umbrella group of information providers. This report summarises the aims, discusses the chief findings and assesses the broader implications of the research.

Curriculum change for the nineties: a report of the Curriculum Development Project on library and information work by E P Dudley et al
LIR Report 14   ISBN 0 7123 3018 6
Part one places the report in its historical context and describes the work which took place. Part two contains the conclusions and recommendations relating to the variety of courses, the content of courses and the constraints on change. The report seeks to promote an informed discussion rather than to prescribe solutions.

The schools information retrieval (SIR) project by M E Rowbottom et al
LIR Report 15   ISBN 0 7123 3020 8
The SIR project was designed to introduce the principles and methods of computerised information retrieval into secondary schools. A microcomputer software package was commissioned and then tested in a variety of secondary schools. The report describes the software and the experiences of each of the schools.

Microcomputer applications in academic libraries by Paul F Burton
LIR Report 16   ISBN 0 7123 3021 6
The report describes the results of a survey of microcomputer use in UK academic libraries carried out in 1982. Details of the hardware and software of many of these libraries are included in the report, as are current and imminent applications. There is also an annotated bibliography on microcomputers and libraries.

The economics of information by John Martyn and A D J Flowerdew
LIR Report 17   ISBN 0 7123 3022 4
A group of economists, accountants and information specialists met in June 1982 to discuss problems in the area of economics of information. This report contains the discussion document circulated to participants before the meeting, the opening address and the final report summarising the discussion.

Local area networks: the implications for library and information science by Mel Collier
LIR Report 19   ISBN 0 7123 3028 3
Local area networks are systems allowing high-speed interconnection of computers within a restricted area. They facilitate distributed processing and indicate a trend away from large, centralised computers. Microcomputer networks are being offered as alternatives to mini-computers for substantial data-processing activities. This report, commissioned in 1982, gives definitions, describes concepts and introduces

some of the techniques involved. The role of local area networks in library and information science is examined, current initiatives are reviewed and finally some suggestions are made for further research in the field.

Inventory of abstracting and indexing services produced in the UK by J Stephens
LIR Report 21   ISBN 0 7123 3030 5
This inventory updates BL R&D Report 5420 of the same title. The entries are arranged alphabetically by name of service. Four indexes are provided: broad subject headings, specific subject headings, an index of responsible authorities, and an index of database processors with the UK online databases they offer.

Information demand and supply in British industry 1977-1983 by The Technical Change Centre
LIR Report 23   ISBN 0 7123 3033 X
Between November 1982 and April 1983 a study was conducted into the effects of the current recession on the supply of technical and commercial information services in British industry. The purpose was to see how industrial information services have adjusted and to investigate how information providers outside industry have reacted to any changes in demand from industry. Questionnaires were distributed among 238 library and information service units in industry, and among 305 external information providers of various kinds. More than half of these provided responses that were analysed. There is evidence that the pattern of demand for, and supply of, information in British industry has changed substantially, and possibly permanently, since 1977.